Praise for *A Principa[l Manager's] Guide to Leverage Le[adership 2.0]*

"If your goal is to become a more strategic practitioner in your conversations, learning experiences, and mentorships, you must have *A Principal Manager's Guide to Leverage Leadership 2.0* in your library! It provides educational leaders at all levels with practical tools to accelerate learning outcomes for students. This book emphasizes what we already know: the real work is done before you even step foot in the classroom! This book has transformed the way I support my school leaders."

—**Celeste Douglas**, assistant superintendent, District 18, New York City Public Schools

"Paul has few peers in the crusade to ensure school leaders have high-fidelity, high-priority practices critical to grow the capacity of their teachers so they can ensure student growth. His latest book fills another void: a clear, detailed map principal supervisors and coaches can use to travel further down the road toward student growth. Inspiring . . . and our school leaders are so thankful!"

—**Rosemary Perlmeter**, founding director, Master's in Urban School Leadership, Southern Methodist University (SMU); cofounder, Teaching Trust; founder, Uplift Education

"Working with Bambrick-Santoyo and the content of this book has been a defining event in my professional life and has made me stronger and better (faster). Following the guidance and protocols set forth in *A Principal Manager's Guide to Leverage Leadership 2.0* helped me strengthen my practice and build the capacity of the leaders I support. Now principal managers have a common language and tools to have a laser-focus on improving the teaching and learning, which can profoundly affect student achievement—as it has for us."

—**Jeanine Zitta**, network superintendent, St. Louis Public Schools

"Whether you are new to supervising principals or have been in the role for years, Paul's work is an invaluable resource to ensuring school leaders get the coaching, tools, and guidance needed to accelerate their schools and take your network of schools to the next level."

—**Sean Precious**, high school instructional superintendent, Denver Public Schools

"The call has been finally been answered. For years principal managers have been searching for the book that helps them prioritize what they should be doing, when they should be doing it, and how often that should occur to have the maximize impact on moving student achievement at schools. Paul has answered these questions and so many more in the most practical and easy-to-understand way. Studying successful leaders across the county, Mr. Bambrick-Santoyo has found a way to make their practices, schedules, routines, and techniques so visible on the pages and in video clips. The trainings and coaching I received from him have shifted my practice more than any other professional development received in my seventeen years in education. The resources in this book changed the way I approached my work in the most profound way possible. My leaders and I were not the same after integrating these practices."

—**LaKimbre Brown**, chief of schools,
Lorain City Schools, Avon Lake, OH

"Paul's powerful insight empowers leaders to overcome challenges and achieve results in manners they did not know was possible. Our partner districts and school systems across the country demonstrate the student impact of leveraging Paul's learning—and this book on principal managers will ignite system changes and results at an even greater scale."

—**William Robinson**, executive director,
Darden/Curry Partnership for Leaders in Education

"Our journey with Paul Bambrick-Santoyo began five years ago, when our school district had six out of the ten worst-performing schools in the state. Paul's first book, *Driven by Data*, became our district bible for school turnaround, followed soon after by the implementation of the seven levers shared in *Leverage Leadership*. Guided by the expertise and experience Paul shares in his books, teachers and leaders have transformed our school district. Now, with this latest book Paul shows more clearly than ever how educators can drive learning through true instructional leadership. I highly recommend this book to anyone who strives to lead a school not as an evaluator, but as a coach."

—**Sandy Coroles**, superintendent, Ogden School District, Ogden, Utah

"Over the years, Paul Bambrick-Santoyo has written a playbook for the world's most difficult job: school and school system leadership. In *A Principal Manager's Guide to Leverage Leadership 2.0*, he shares this playbook and—more important—explains *exactly* how to use it. If you and your team care about teaching and learning, you'll want this book and you'll use it every single day."

—**Charlie Friedman**, founder and head of school,
Nashville Classical Charter Schools

A Principal Manager's Guide to
LEVERAGE LEADERSHIP 2.0

How to Build Exceptional Schools
Across Your District

Paul Bambrick-Santoyo

JB JOSSEY-BASS™

A Wiley Brand

Published by Jossey-Bass

A Wiley Brand
One Montgomery Street, Suite 1000, San Francisco, CA 94104-4594—www.josseybass.com

Library of Congress Cataloging-in-Publication Data has been applied for.

ISBN 978-1-119-49664-9 (pbk); ISBN 978-1-119-49667-0 (ePDF); ISBN 978-1-119-49665-6 (epub)

Cover image: © Veer
Cover design: Wiley

Printed in the United States of America

FIRST EDITION

PB Printing V10010681_060519

Contents

PART 2 How to Coach

PART 3 Systems

DVD Video Content

Here is an overview of the video clips for your quick reference.

Identifying the Right Action Steps (Chapter 2)

Clip	Technique	Description	Page
1	See It and Name It—Manager Feedback Meeting	**"What is the purpose of plan before practice?"** Jeanine Zitta works with Principal Glass to analyze a gap in the facilitation of the principal's feedback meetings, ultimately prompting the leader to identify a final action step to implement in the immediate future.	28

Coaching Data-Driven Instruction (Chapter 3)

Clip	Technique	Description	Page
2	See It (Exemplar)—Weekly Data Meeting	**"This is a meaty standard."** LaKimbre Brown leads her principal team to unpack a third-grade math standard around multiplication.	72, 107
3	See It (Gap)—Weekly Data Meeting	**"Using the language of the standard ..."** Juliana Worrell works with principal Jacobi Clifton and his third-grade teachers during a weekly data meeting to determine the highest-leverage gap, utilizing the charts of the standard and the exemplar to target and fix the conceptual misconception.	108

Clip	Technique	Description	Page
4	**See It and Name It—Weekly Data Meetings**	**"I would add something else."** Juliana Worrell asks principal Na'Jee Carter to analyze the standard and the exemplar, prompting Na'Jee to fully unpack the characteristics of his own written exemplar in order to prepare him to lead the same data meeting with his teachers.	108
5	**Do It (Plan)— Weekly Data Meetings**	**"Now it's time to spar."** Juliana Worrell plans a reteach lesson side by side with Na'Jee Carter, and then they compare their plans to determine strengths and next steps.	108
6	**See It and Do It— Coach by Doing**	**"What are the actions that you would want to see replicated?"** Juliana Worrell leads principal Andrew Schaeffer to fully unpack his school's exemplar for guided reading before determining the highest-leverage gap across several guided reading classrooms.	110, 111
7	**Name It—Coach by Doing**	**"Reflect on the process: your key takeaways are . . ."** Juliana Worrell pauses her modeling of a literacy weekly data meeting with principal Na'Jee Carter to ask him to reflect on key takeaways and name his action step for his upcoming data meeting.	112
8	**Follow Up— Manager Feedback Meeting**	**"I am going to send you the third-grade analysis meeting."** Julie Jackson works with principal Jennifer Wong-Den to list all of the time-bound next steps at the conclusion of the meeting.	113

Coaching Student Culture (Chapter 4)

Clip	Technique	Description	Page
9*	Do It—Practice Clinic	**"Take one minute to read the technique."** Hannah Lofthus's principals lead a morning practice clinic to improve teacher actions before the school day begins.	128
10	Do It—Roll Out to Staff (Principal Clip)	**"Handshake, high-five, or hug . . ."** Tera Carr begins her student culture rollout by presenting the model to her staff.	131
11	See It and Name It	**"Here's what you are going to see me do."** Hannah Lofthus presents a model for her principal to compare to his own implementation, prompting the principal to name both his coaches' action step and his own.	131
12	Do It (Coach by Walking)	**". . . and then we are going to go upstairs and do it."** Jesse Corburn asks principal Ashley Anderson to practice the planned real-time feedback before their school walkthrough.	137
13	Do It (Coach by Walking)	**" Whisper to him that you're going to watch for . . ."** Jesse Corburn provides Ashley with several opportunities to practice real-time feedback aligned to her action step.	137
14	See It and Name It (Coach by Meeting)	**"What is the gap between [what you described as the ideal] and what we saw today?"** Hannah Loftus pushes her principal to identify the exemplar procedure for her dean to follow when receiving a student, and then they determine the gap in the current implementation coupled with a final action step.	139
15	Do It (Coach by Meeting)	**"She'll be able to implement that within the next thirty minutes."** Hannah Loftus practices the principal action step with her leader during a feedback meeting.	140

---

*This clip is an additional resource that was created after the creation of the DVD. To access it, use the following Vimeo link: https://vimeo.com/264996206.

Coaching Teams of Principals (Chapter 5)

DVD Additional Materials

Here is quick overview of additional materials available on the DVD.

Resource	Description
Principal Manager Quick Reference Guide	Key one-pagers and guides to support the coaching of principals; these can be printed and formed into a small reference guide for each principal manager: • Leverage Leadership Sequence of Action Steps for Principals • Principal Manager Check-In one-pager • Managing Principals to Results one-pager • Weekly Data Meeting one-pager • Giving Effective Feedback one-pager • Real-Time Feedback one-pager • Student Culture one-pager • Leading PD one-pager • Get Better Faster Scope and Sequence of Action Steps
Leverage Leadership Quick Reference Guide for Principals	Key one-pagers and guides for every lever; these can be printed and formed into a small reference guide for each principal: • Weekly Data Meeting one-pager • Giving Effective Feedback one-pager

Resource	Description
	• Real-Time Feedback one-pager • Student Culture one-pager • Leading PD one-pager • Get Better Faster Scope and Sequence of Action Steps • Get Better Faster Coach's Guide
PD Session: Data-Driven Instruction for Principal Managers	All the materials needed to lead a professional development session for instructional leaders on data-driven instruction • Session plan • PowerPoint presentation • Handouts • One-pagers
Implementation Materials for Data-Driven Instruction	Key handouts to support the implementation of data-driven instruction, including: • Network dashboard sample • School dashboard sample • Managing Principals to Results one-pager • Weekly-Daily Data Meeting one-pager • Principal Manager Check-In one-pager
PD Session: Leading Student Culture for Principal Managers	All the materials needed to lead a professional development session for instructional leaders on student culture • Session plan • PowerPoint presentation • Handouts • One-pagers
Implementation Materials for Culture	Key handouts to support the implementation of student culture, including: • 30-Day Playbook • Student Culture Rubric • Student Culture one-pager

Resource	Description
Implementation Materials for Finding the Time	Key handouts to help principal managers find the time for what matters most, including: • Weekly Schedule Template
Leverage Leadership Evaluation Rubrics	Leverage Leadership Instructional Leadership (non-principal) Rubric Leverage Leadership Principal Evaluation Rubric

For leaders of leaders: your children are my children.

Acknowledgments

I didn't really know what was possible for principal managers until I got a chance to see each of you in action: Tamara Acevedo, Kevin Anderle, Nikki Bridges, Laura Brinkman, LaKimbre Brown, Lamont Browne, Dan Caeser, Colleen Colarusso, Brian Conley, Denise de la Rosa, Monica Dilts Nurrenbern, Tatiana Epanchin, Hope Evans, Charlie Friedman, Laura Garza, Jessee Haight, Shara Hegde, Sondra Jolovich-Motes, Teresa Khirallah, Ben Klompus, Hannah Lofthus, Ben Marcovitz, Doug McCurry, Erin McMahon, Adam Meinig, Gina Musumeci, Sultana Noormuhamad, Sabrina Pence, Ciji Pittman, Sean Precious, Jesse Rector, Eric Sanchez, Stacey Shells, David Singer, Billy Snow, Chi Tschang, Rebecca Utton, Nicole Veltze, Alison Welcher, Jeanine Zitta, and Josh Zoia. This book wouldn't have happened if not for the work you're doing all across the country. Thank you for modeling for me and for inspiring me to write this book.

Jesse Corburn, Juliana Worrell, Kelly Dowling, Serena Savarirayan, Maya Roth Bisignano, Katie Yezzi, and J.T. Leaird: we wouldn't have been able to take these ideas far and wide without proving them at home first. Thanks for every moment watching video, perfecting practice, and discovering new ways to be better. The seeds of your work are bearing fruit.

Julie Jackson: sixteen years working side by side—now that is a gift I will always cherish.

Alyssa Ross: on the spur of the moment I asked you to take on the challenge of working on not one but two books simultaneously, and you did not shy away. Thank you for the creativity, the sparring, and the writing companionship. Here's to a continuing ride on the wave of writing.

Brett Peiser, Josh Phillips, Diane Flynn, Laura Lee McGovern, Sara Batterton, Sam Messer, Sam Tweedy, Jacque Rauschuber, Young Rhee, Michael Ambriz, Anna Hall,

Tara Marlovitz, Doug Lemov, Erica Woolway, and Angelica Gonzalez Pastoriza: you have supported me even when I have been difficult and overdemanding, and you quietly transform everything I do from dream to reality. Thanks for being the wind that makes flight possible.

Lindsay Kruse, Kathleen Sullivan, and Norman Atkins: you saw a dream with me, and the Leverage Leadership Institute was born. It is hard to believe how far we've come! Keep soaring.

David Deatherage: you were the lone ranger on this one, from the early principal manager working groups to the filming and cutting of footage of managers in action. Thank you for never losing your passion and enthusiasm—it is contagious!

Ana, Maria, and Nicolas: you have my heart—always. Follow your dreams (you already have).

Gaby: twenty-one years and it still feels fresh and new. I'm so excited to spend another twenty-one years together—and then some. Here's to warmth, bright skies, and getting old together.

Thank you to each and every one of you. This book is a tribute to you all.

About the Author

Paul Bambrick-Santoyo is the chief schools officer for Uncommon Schools and the founder and dean of the Leverage Leadership Institute, creating proof points of excellence in urban schools nationwide. Author of *Driven by Data*; *Leverage Leadership*; *Great Habits, Great Readers*; and *Get Better Faster*; Bambrick-Santoyo has trained more than twenty thousand school leaders worldwide in instructional leadership, including multiple schools that have gone on to become the highest-gaining or highest-achieving schools in their districts, states, and/or countries. Prior to these roles, Bambrick-Santoyo cofounded the Relay National Principals Academy Fellowship and spent thirteen years leading North Star Academies in Newark, New Jersey. During his tenure at North Star, the schools grew from serving fewer than three hundred students to over three thousand while at the same time making dramatic gains in student achievement. North Star's results make them among the highest-achieving urban schools in the nation and winners of multiple recognitions, including the US Department of Education's National Blue Ribbon Award. Prior to his work at North Star, Bambrick-Santoyo worked for six years in a bilingual school in Mexico City, where he founded the International Baccalaureate program. He earned a BA in social justice from Duke University and his MEd in school administration through New Leaders from the City University of New York—Baruch College.

Introduction

By any metric, John Williams is an iconic creator of music. In a career that spans five decades and counting, Williams has composed some of the most unforgettable film scores of all time, including six *Star Wars* films, three *Harry Potter* films, and the chill-inducing "dah-*dah*—dah-*dah*" of *Jaws*.[1] His notes shaped these stories into the masterpieces we know them as today, making his mark on cinematic history as indelible as his mark on music.

This legendary skill of composing is combined with Williams's skill in leading others to perform. He served as the conductor of the Boston Pops Orchestra for thirteen years, and continues to occasionally serve as conductor for the Pops, at the London Symphony, and at the Hollywood Bowl.[2] These performances are extraordinarily popular—not only because of Williams's fame as a composer but also because of his work as a conductor. He excels at leading other musicians to perform memorable music—sometimes his own art, but sometimes music crafted by others—in a breathtaking way.

Step back and think about Williams's impact in the moment he lifts a conductor's baton. He doesn't play a single instrument; he doesn't offer a single bit of sound to what is produced. Yet there is no performance without him. Even as he hands the task of making the music over to other artists, the audience depends on Williams to thrill them with wonder, terror, or delight.

The same is true of every principal manager. You're no longer in the classroom, and you're no longer in one school every day. You're no longer welcoming a student body in the morning or holding regular feedback meetings with teachers, but you work daily to make sure every school succeeds.

Just like a conductor, you no longer make the music—but there is no performance without you.

Core Idea

As the conductor, you no longer make the music,
but there is no performance without you.

As principal managers, we can sometimes lose sight of the power of the conductor's coaching. We can get so mired in the complexities of multischool leadership that we can feel distant and ineffective—and sometimes that feeling becomes a reality. Yet a new generation of principal managers shows that this does not have to be the case: people like LaKimbre Brown in Washington, DC; Hannah Lofthus in Kansas City; Teresa Khirallah in Dallas; Jeanine Zitta in St. Louis; and Serena Savarirayan and Juliana Worrell in Newark, New Jersey. All of them had significant success as principals, but what is more remarkable is the success they now have as managers. Between them, they have worked with nearly every type of school—small and large, district and charter, schools in turnaround and schools moving from good to great. In each context, they have changed the lives of whole communities of students. No matter what the odds or difficulties, principal managers can indeed make the difference in the schools they manage, creating amazing music by guiding and coaching the musicians.

How do they do it?

That is what this book is all about.

A PARADIGM SHIFT: FROM ADMINISTRATION TO INSTRUCTION

What makes education effective? Great teaching.[3] What makes great teaching possible across an entire school? Great principals.

Leverage Leadership 2.0 was built to codify the practices of the most effective school leaders across the country. But in the process of working with schools leaders in every type of district, another question emerged: What does it actually look like to make great schools possible at scale? More specifically, what do the best principal managers do?

For most of us who have risen to the role of principal manager, we got there by being a good principal. But just as being a good student doesn't prepare you to be a good teacher, neither does the work of being principal fully prepare you to manage other principals. Think again of John Williams: the skills he engages when he stands up to conduct are fully different from those he uses when he plays an instrument.

Among principal managers whom I've met along my journey, a common refrain is, "Nothing prepared me to be a principal manager. In all honesty, I don't really know if what I'm doing is making any impact." In large measure there is a void in the field: there is little training offered to guide us in being principal managers. That's where this book comes in.

Just as student learning won't change if we don't improve instruction, our work as principal managers won't change until we make the shift from being administrators to serving as instructional leaders. Why? Because at its core, being an instructional leader means believing that principals can get better. They aren't born great; they can grow into becoming great. This entails a paradigm shift: moving from simply monitoring or evaluating school leaders to coaching them.[4]

Core Idea

The purpose of principal managers is not to monitor or evaluate school leaders but to develop them.
Good principals don't have to be born great; they can become great.

Obstacles to Effective School Management

As promising as this shift sounds on paper, there are many obstacles that make it challenging to put into practice. Here are a few of the most fundamental ones.

- **A fixed mindset about schools—and school leaders.** For many of us who were principals before we became principal managers, we never got any feedback as a principal. We found our own way. That experience can leave us believing that the next generation of principals can do the same. Once they know about teaching, surely they can figure out how to lead, right? This mindset leads to deprioritizing giving principals the feedback and information they need to grow. It can also lead to a more dangerous proposition: the belief that a struggling principal will never be able to get better, and thus that principal's school is destined to fail. Only when we shift from this fixed mindset to a growth mindset about our schools' leaders can we begin to change our actions to coach principals to mastery. (The terms *fixed mindset* and *growth mindset* were coined by Carol S. Dweck in her seminal book *Mindset: The New Psychology of Success*.)

- **A focus on compliance and administration.** One of the largest stumbling blocks principal managers face today in their journey to becoming instructional leaders is the sheer volume of noninstructional work placed on their shoulders—nearly the exact problem principals face at the school level. All too often, principal managers find themselves focused on a host of tasks far removed from directly improving instruction and learning: attending district meetings, learning the latest around compliance, planning a budget or managing non-school-based staff, just to name a few. This work is not going to disappear, and often principal managers are evaluated more for getting that work done well than they are for their schools' results. Such tasks have led some to argue that a great superintendent or principal manager should focus on being good at these things and leave instructional leadership to principals and coaches. However, what I saw in exceptional principal managers was an insistence on being instructional leaders. No matter the other responsibilities they had on their plate, a focus on teaching and learning always rose to the top.

- **Firefighter syndrome—letting the urgent crowd out the important.** When you lead multiple schools, there will always be something urgent that pushes you to abandon every well-laid plan. You have multiple "fires" to extinguish—from disciplinary hearings to personnel challenges to occasionally things far worse. You end up rushing from one fire to the next, yet you arrive unprepared and ill-equipped to address them. And with each fire, instructional leadership falls even further into the shadows.

- **Flying at too high an altitude to effect real change on the ground.** Many times principal managers try to manage from far away. They create plans and roll them out, but they do not follow up with "boots on the ground" to actually manage, model, and monitor the implementation. Redefining management as on-the-ground support makes the difference between running great schools in theory and making that a reality.

- **Inertia that supports the status quo.** All of the challenges I've described here lead us to a sense of inertia whereby we can start to lose hope that any other way is possible. And given that we don't have a model of an alternative, we get stuck—mired in the work of administration.

The Seven Levers: A Pathway to Instructional Leadership

The leaders highlighted in this book face the same obstacles, but they overcome them. They follow a core set of principles that allow for consistent, transformational, and replicable growth across their schools. They start by taking advantage of the common language and tools of *Leverage Leadership 2.0* to create a platform on which they can form and develop their principals for success. These are truly levers that answer the core question of school leadership: What should an effective school leader do?

The Seven Levers

Instructional Levers

1. **Data-driven instruction.** Define the road map for rigor and adapt teaching to meet students' needs.
2. **Instructional planning.** Plan backwards to guarantee strong lessons.
3. **Observation and feedback.** Coach teachers to improve the learning.
4. **Professional development.** Strengthen culture and instruction with hands-on training that sticks.

Cultural Levers

5. **Student culture.** Create a strong culture where learning can thrive.
6. **Staff culture.** Build and support the right team.
7. **Managing school leadership teams.** Train instructional leaders to expand your impact across the school.

By focusing on these levers and leveraging the power of a common framework, the principal managers highlighted in this book were able to dramatically improve the performance of their school leaders—and themselves. But how do you coach principals around these levers? This book will offer you the tools to do so and, in turn, take your schools to new heights.

A "PRACTICAL GUIDE": WHAT YOU'LL FIND IN THE BOOK

In the pages that follow, we will offer a concrete, step-by-step guide to becoming an excellent principal manager. The book is organized into four sections:

- **What to coach:** a primer on the seven levers of leadership (for those who are not deeply familiar with *Leverage Leadership 2.0*) and an introduction to the trajectory of actions steps for a principal's development

- **How to coach:** a deep dive into coaching principals, both one-on-one and in teams, with a particular focus on the two "super-levers" (the most important for student achievement): data-driven instruction and student culture

- **Systems:** how to build your schedule and create district-wide conditions for success that maximize your time on instructional leadership

- **How to coach the principal managers:** a full set of materials—session plans, PowerPoints, and handouts—for you to roll out training for other principal managers on your team

Within each of these sections, we use the See It, Name It, Do It approach to present the content of the book.

See It: Videos and Testimonials

Videos

In the DVD that accompanies this text, we've included a selection of video clips of principal managers in action, working directly with their principals. This is a gold mine for you, as there are few, if any, resources like this available for principal managers. These videos are not staged, nor are they videos of managers' interactions with their strongest principals. These videos show principal manager interactions with all types of principals: struggling principals, new principals, and those at every level.

In this sense, we bring these schools to you: every chapter is accompanied by high-quality video of the lever it presents, broken down to portray both the components of success and how it looks as a whole. Seeing exactly what the leaders in this book do, and how they do it, will make it possible to replicate their actions in a way that reading alone never could.

Throughout the book, this symbol indicates that a given video clip on the DVD is crucial to the work and to the reading itself. Although it is possible to use this book without watching the accompanying video, we doubt it will be as effective. Watching exemplars of great leadership in practice will provide insights that words will not. These are also at the foundation of the training materials in Chapter 8 and on the DVD (more on that presently).

Name It: Core Ideas and One-Pagers

The power of a common language to describe best practices is impossible to overstate. Here's how this book serves to provide one, naming the most important actions that lead to the results we need the most.

Core Ideas

Throughout the text, these Core Idea boxes will pull out the most important key ideas from each section.

> ### Core Idea
>
> If standards are meaningless until you define how to assess them, then principal management is directionless without district-wide quality interim assessments.

The goal of each core idea is to make the complex ideas in this book as simple and as memorable as possible. If you take nothing else away from this reading, take these—and share them with those you work with!

One-Pagers and Summary Guides

We have routinely received feedback that the one-pagers and summary guides to specific skills are among the most useful tools in the book to implement best practices across your school leaders. These one-pagers aren't invented from thin air. Carefully built and concise, they simply name the key words and actions we observed in thousands of hours of observations and video clips of the most effective principal managers. They consolidate the most important information to remember about any topic onto a few pages. The following is an excerpt from the Principal Manager Check-In one-pager in Chapter 3.

Do It	Do It: Plan, Practice, Follow Up
	Principal Manager Check-In A Guide for Developing Principals One-on-One

Do It	Do It: Plan, Practice, Follow Up
	Plan before practice: • Script the changes into upcoming plans (for meetings or observations) o "Where would be a good place and time to implement this next week?" o "What are all the actions you need to take/want to see in the teachers?" o "Take three minutes to write up your plan." • Push to make the plan more precise and more detailed. o "What prompts will you use with teachers that we can practice today?" o "Now that you've made your initial plan, what will do you if [key challenge: e.g., resistant teacher]?" • (If struggling to make a strong plan) Model for the leader and debrief. o "Watch what I do and say as I model __." "What do you notice about how I did __?" • Perfect the plan. o "Those three steps look great. Let's add __ to your [script/meeting plan]."

This book includes key guidance in every chapter and full one-pagers and summary guides on the DVD. Print them out and use them as a daily guide in your work—and distribute them among your peer principal managers so that they can do the same!

Do It: Materials to Make It Happen

It is one thing to have a guide; it is another to be able to roll this out. *A Principal Manager's Guide to Leverage Leadership 2.0* includes all the same tools that the leaders in this book use to lift the levers in their schools.

Action Planning

Throughout each chapter, we give you the space to evaluate the quality of your own leadership and to plan when and how you'll put these ideas into action. This sort of self-evaluation and strategic work is what makes meaningful change possible. In boxes labeled "Stop and Jot" or "Action Planning Worksheet," you'll find sets of questions designed for you to assess your current principal management, choose the resources from the book that will be most helpful, and plan your first action steps. Here is an example.

Pulling the Lever: Action Planning Worksheet

Coaching Principals on Data-Driven Instruction

Network/District Assessment

- Review the district conditions for successful implementation of data-driven instruction (as discussed in the first section of the chapter): Which are the key actions you need to take as a network of schools?

_____

_____

_____

_____

Self-Assessment

- Review the Leverage Leadership Sequence of Action Steps for Principals (embedded throughout the chapter; the full list can be found at the end of Chapter 2, and a print-friendly version is in the DVD appendix).
- Which action steps do you want to target this year as you develop your principals?

_____

_____

_____

_____

Planning for Action

- What tools from this book will you use to lead your schools? Check all that you will use. (All are available on the DVD unless noted otherwise.)
  - ☐ Network dashboard sample
  - ☐ School dashboard sample
  - ☐ Managing Principals to Results one-pager
  - ☐ Weekly Data Meeting one-pager
  - ☐ Principal Manager Check-In one-pager
  - ☐ PD on data-driven instruction for principal managers
  - ☐ PD on data-driven instruction for principals (see *Driven by Data*)
  - ☐ Other: _____

- How will you modify these resources to meet your district's needs?

  _____

  _____

  _____

- What are your next steps for coaching principals on data-driven instruction?

Action	Date

Professional Development Materials

Finally, we want you to be able to use this book not just for yourself but with your fellow principal managers. We have therefore included materials for two full days of workshops for principal managers around coaching principals in the levers of data-driven instruction and student culture. These materials are nicely supplemented by all the PD materials provided in *Leverage Leadership 2.0.*

WHO SHOULD USE THIS BOOK—AND HOW

This book is for principal managers, but who exactly are principal managers? On the most obvious level, principal managers are people who are responsible for the success of more than one school. That applies to a large range of titles that vary by district and organization: superintendents, assistant superintendents, school chiefs, executive directors—this list is endless! Yet if this book is about creating effective schools at scale, then the "circle of leadership" extends not only to those roles but also to school boards, state departments of education, principal training organizations, school turnaround programs, and any organization devoted to developing school leaders. If your role is to make principals better, then this book is for you.

For the purpose of simplicity of the narrative, we will refer to these leaders as "principal managers." "Principal instructional leaders" would be more apropos—but it's also more of a tongue twister.

As we will note throughout the book, the methods we offer have worked in some of the most challenging conditions in American education. The fact that our case studies are drawn from underserved urban areas is no accident; the schools and students who most need dramatic change are those that are currently least well served. Yet although our main setting is urban schools, the systems we propose here, when used well, can generate significant impact in any school.

How to Read the Book—Principal Managers

The order in which you will implement this leadership model will depend on you—your needs and your schools' level of progress. Here are some global recommendations.

Step 1: Get Familiar with the Leverage Leadership Model

Chapter 1 is a primer on the Leverage Leadership model and can serve as your starting point. It is very difficult to talk about school management until we have established a common language about what excellent instructional leadership looks like, and it is impossible to coach leaders in that language if we don't know it ourselves. If you have more time, a full read of *Leverage Leadership 2.0* can give you a more complete guide and set of resources to the best practices of leaders across the country as they've used the levers of leadership—and it includes many important revisions and updates to the original *Leverage Leadership*. If you have already read *Leverage Leadership 2.0*, you can skip Chapter 1.

Step 2: Read Chapters 2–5—What and How to Coach

Chapter 2 introduces you to the Leverage Leadership Sequence of Action Steps for Principals a trajectory of action steps for a principal's development. Very similar to the Get Better Faster sequence of action steps for teachers found in *Get Better Faster: A Coach's Guide to Developing New Teachers*, this sequence focuses on principal-level action steps and is the foundation for the book. Chapters 3–5 dive into the core work of instructional leadership of principals.

Step 3: Build Your Schedule and Systems with Chapter 6

The most important factor that separates exceptional school leaders from the rest is the intentional use of their time. Chapter 6 walks you through how to rebuild your personal schedule—and build systems around it to maximize the amount and quality of time you spend on instructional leadership. Do not skip this chapter: without the right schedule, none of the steps captured in the previous chapters will come to fruition.

Step 4: Use the PD Materials as Needed

Part 4 is not really meant to be read but to be used: it contains the facilitators' guides for training other principal managers in school management. Use them whenever you need to in order to train fellow principal managers.

How to Read the Book—Superintendents and Central Office and State Leadership

If you are the superintendent of a larger district who does not manage principals directly but rather manages principal managers, or if you work at the central office or at the state or regional level of leadership, consider the following reading plan:

- **Step 1: Get familiar with the Leverage Leadership model.** Just as for principal managers, Chapter 1 is a primer on the Leverage Leadership model. If you have more time, reading *Leverage Leadership 2.0* can give you a more comprehensive understanding.

- **Step 2: Read the Superintendent's Guide (Chapter 7).** Chapter 7 will be the most important chapter for you: how to create the conditions for success at the district level so that your principals and principal managers can fly. A lot of the work will be about blocking and tackling to allow instructional leadership to be the predominant work of your leaders.

- **Step 3: Read the schedules and systems for principal managers (Chapter 6).** Chapter 6 will make sure you have a clear vision for how your principal managers should schedule their time.

- **Step 4: Read everything else.** This will enable you to see the nuts and bolts of what you'll want your principal managers to do on a daily basis. Part 4 will be particularly valuable as it gives you the facilitator's guides for training all your principal managers.

THE PATH AHEAD

It wasn't that long ago—May 2013—that someone approached me to ask when I would take the time to start developing resources and materials for principal managers. I still remember the words of the first person who approached me with this topic, a superintendent from a fairly small district. He had just attended one of my workshops on data-driven instruction, and he said, "I love the guidance for schools, but I really want to hear about what I can do in my role as principal manager. Everyone assumes we know what we're doing, and we really don't. Please help fill the void!"

Those comments launched a journey in studying the most effective principal managers I could find—and trying to implement their practices myself as well. Over the course of that work, I saw firsthand the overwhelming challenges facing principal managers—but I also saw leaders who are bright lights showing us the way.

This book is about the action steps behind those shining lights. It's about a cohort of leaders who have taken effective school leadership to a larger number of schools. Each one of our schools is unique, yet there is also a commonality in the solutions we can use to support them.

It is important to recognize that these improvements demand hard work. But one thing we've noticed across the country is that most school leaders already work very hard. The power of these steps is that they help you work "smart"—they lock in the results you strive for and that your students deserve.

Part 1

What to Coach

Chapter 1

A Primer on Leverage Leadership

 Stop Here

This chapter is a primer on the seven levers of leadership as captured in *Leverage Leadership 2.0.* If you have already read *Leverage Leadership 2.0,* feel free to skip this chapter. Reading *Leverage Leadership 2.0* before you dive into this book will give you the most complete understanding of this book, as it will give you common language to describe the best practices of effective principals. However, if time is not on your side, we offer this primer to you. So, depending on your level of familiarity with *Leverage Leadership 2.0,* skip to Chapter 2 or keep reading!

Lifting the Super-Levers

August 2017: The Student Culture Rehearsal

Annie Webb Blanton Elementary School looks ready for the beginning of a school day. It's 7:30 a.m., teachers are placing a healthy breakfast on each desk, and desks are arranged with a brightly colored name tag for every student. Those seats are even occupied—but not by the students. That's because it's 7:30 a.m. several days *before* school starts, and the staff of Blanton are on campus to rehearse exactly what they'll have to do when the students arrive to make sure everything goes smoothly.

Walking up and down the halls is principal Laura Garza, praising her staff for what they're already getting right—and delivering quick feedback on what she wants to see improved by the real Day 1. "Nice posture," she tells fourth-grade teacher Tania Fuentes, smiling. At another classroom door, she points to a teacher who is playing the role of a reluctant student, prompting that "student's" teacher, Nancy Cazares, to address her behavior.

After the staff has rehearsed the entire breakfast routine, Laura pauses the rehearsal and brings her teachers together. "How did what we practice reflect the action plan we named when we first rolled out our breakfast routine?" she asks her team. One teacher, Emily Sapoch, shares that rehearsing the breakfast routine so quickly made her realize how efficient it was, and how it would set a tone of urgency for the whole school day. Nancy—the same teacher whom Laura prompted to make a behavioral correction—says that clear expectations of what students should be doing during breakfast made it easier to know what to say and do during a redirect.

Laura beams. "Excellent," she says. "Well done, everyone! Let's move into the next phase of our rehearsal. On my signal, transition to classrooms!"

October 2017: The Weekly Data Meeting

A few months into the school year, Laura Garza is meeting with her first-grade team. Each teacher has come prepared with recent samples of student work, which they're now reviewing together.

One teacher, Katherine Dominick, excitedly shares that most of the students in her class who have been struggling with a new guided reading skill—keeping track of character change in a story—have now mastered it. "What seemed to make the difference was prompting them to state how the character was different at the beginning versus the end," she says. Another teacher, Mauricio Garcia, says this prompt has been effective in his classroom as well, and everyone has the opportunity to share the progress his or her students have made since the previous week's data meeting.

Laura joins in celebrating these successes with her teachers, pointing out that the strategies students are now able to use successfully reflect that they have overcome a key conceptual misunderstanding that had been holding them back from mastering standards. "We flagged last week that they were having trouble keeping track of changes over the course of the story, and now they're improving," she says. "Well done, everyone! Now let's take a look at the students who are still struggling with this. What is the gap between what these successful students are doing and what's happening with the students who still aren't comprehending?"

For the next two minutes, teachers quietly look back over incorrect student work, looking for key conceptual misunderstandings. Then they share out, pooling their knowledge about their students to find the best next steps. Katherine comments, "The root issue might be that they're still struggling with cause and effect—that's something we flagged for both Sofia and Victor earlier in the year."

The group nods, and Laura asks: "So how should we reteach this: modeling or guided discourse?" For the remainder of the meeting, the team makes a plan to close the gap they've identified—one that will support their students right away.

Laura Garza's goals for her students are easy for her to sum up. "I want to show them they can learn," she says. "I want them to believe in themselves."

But as many were all too quick to warn Laura, that's easier said than done. When Laura became principal of Annie Webb Blanton Elementary School in 2015, less than half of her students were achieving at grade level for either math or literacy. Laura was determined to get them on track quickly: conscious of the time they'd already lost in their education careers, she wanted to see improvement within a year. Several naysayers told Laura this wouldn't be possible—that her students, the overwhelming majority of whom were Latino students who not only qualified for a free or reduced lunch but also were English language learners, were too set back by "behavioral problems" to achieve what Laura wanted for them.

These stories didn't discourage Laura; they bolstered her resolution. She realized that if she wanted her students to believe they could learn, she'd have to do more than believe in them herself: she'd have to make sure they really *did* learn, and quickly. So, during the summer, she trained her staff in the cultural systems that would make Blanton a safe place to learn; and when the school year got started, she met with teachers every week to check students' progress toward their learning goals.

Laura says the changes started to show on Day 1. Thanks to rehearsals like the one we saw in the opening of this chapter, expectations for students and staff alike were crystal clear from the door. "Honestly, Day 1 was amazing," Laura reflects now. "Children were coming in and being greeted by their teachers—it was really beautiful. And it just kept getting better."

Blanton has continued to get better ever since. By the end of two years, student learning had skyrocketed (see Figure 1.1).[1]

It should come as no surprise that Laura was Dallas Principal of the Year as evidence of her outstanding achievement.

Laura is far from the only educator who has heard that her students aren't capable of learning, but she's also not the only one proving that kind of thinking wrong. In fact, at the time of this writing, more than twenty thousand leaders worldwide have implemented the practices that have made Laura successful, with success stories from coast to coast and from Chile to South Africa. None of these leaders are miracle workers. Rather, what they all have in common is how they spend their time—and how they lead others to do the same.

Core Idea

Exceptional school leaders succeed because of how they use their time:
what they do and when they do it.

Figure 1.1 Texas State Assessment (STAAR): Blanton Elementary School, Percentage at or Above Proficiency

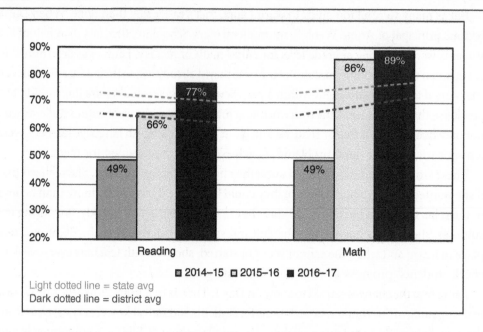

The Leverage Leadership model is about implementing replicable strategies used by leaders like Laura to manage their time in a way that drives learning—however challenging the circumstances. It boils down to seven key sets of actions: the seven levers of leadership. Whether you're a school leader or a leader of leaders, spending your time on these will ensure that you spend your time on what matters most for the children you serve.

THE SEVEN LEVERS OF LEADERSHIP

Consider the performance of an outstanding athletic team. When you watch an effective team like the University of Connecticut's women's basketball team—the most successful program in collegiate history—you can describe what it looks like at game time: you might notice the superstars, but what's even more striking is how well all players work in unison. The offensive plays expose the gaps in the opponent's defense, the footwork is precise, the passing is phenomenal, and every player makes a maximal impact.

But no one can replicate this success just by watching the game. The difference comes in each player's understanding of what she has to do. The point guard has to read the defense and determine where to break it down with either dribble penetration or an effective pass. The shooting guards have to rotate through their teammate's picks to isolate them for an open shot. And the forwards and centers must take up precise positions underneath the basket to receive a pass or get a crucial rebound. Each one knows the precise moment when she has to move or shoot or pass, based on thousands of drills done in practice. In essence, the team has a detailed step-by-step plan that is capable of adjusting to what happens in the moment.

Let's posit that in schools and school districts, just as on athletic teams, each team member must know what actions he or she must take to lead to victory for all. What, then, are school leaders doing concretely each moment that makes their schools function exceptionally? What are the actions that lead not to just somewhat effective learning but to phenomenal results from every teacher? What do these leaders prioritize on a day-by-day, minute-by-minute schedule?

In observing the most successful school leaders over the past decade, we've named those key actions as seven levers—the levers that catapult achievement forward. They are data-driven instruction, planning, observation and feedback, professional development, student culture, staff culture, and managing leadership teams.

THE SEVEN LEVERS

Instructional Levers

1. **Data-driven instruction.** Define the road map for rigor and adapt teaching to meet students' needs.
2. **Instructional planning.** Plan backwards to guarantee strong lessons.
3. **Observation and feedback.** Coach teachers to improve the learning.
4. **Professional development.** Strengthen culture and instruction with hands-on training that sticks.

Cultural Levers

5. **Student culture.** Create a strong culture where learning can thrive.
6. **Staff culture.** Build and support the right team.
7. **Managing school leadership teams.** Train instructional leaders to expand your impact across the school.

Each of the seven levers is essential to running a great school, and for principals, narrowing your focus to these is game-changing. As a principal manager, you can't take full charge of every one of them at every school you're responsible for—you will need to narrow your focus to the levers that matter most for each leader at his or her stage of development.

In this book, we'll focus primarily on the two super-levers that, as Laura discovered, matter the most for school growth: data-driven instruction (ensure students are learning what they need) and student culture (build an environment where that learning is possible). But the actions described in coaching principals can be applied to every lever.

How? There is a simple, universal way to coach: See It. Name It. Do It.

SEE IT. NAME IT. DO IT.

There's a well-loved proverb in literary circles to the effect that a writer works in the dark, until a reader comes along and turns on the light. That has certainly been true of codifying the Leverage Leadership model. When we published *Leverage Leadership* in 2012, based on the experiences of thousands of school leaders across the country, we described each of the seven levers distinctly with its own language. However, as more and more leaders read *Leverage Leadership* or attended professional development on the practices it advocates, thousands of leaders became tens of thousands, and a unifying framework began to illuminate what it really takes to implement each of these levers. The power of this unifying approach can best be illustrated by my experience learning to cook cod.

When I was growing up, I never liked fish. Fast-forward years later to my first year living in Mexico City: my father-in-law, Miguel, prepared a delicious cod dish called Bacalao a la Mexicana. I was hooked! But I had no idea how to prepare it myself. I watched Miguel cook it once and wrote down the ingredients, but when I got around to cooking it myself, I couldn't remember the details. So I watched him again, this time noting the subtleties and writing them down: strain the diced tomatoes before adding to the mix, skim the water off the top, and continue cooking until only oil is bubbling along the edges of the pot. I asked Miguel to watch me, and he let me cook, just adding subtle tips. Sure enough, I was successful (although not quite as good as Miguel himself).

My experience in the kitchen mirrors what we saw when observing instructional leadership. Each lever boils down to a core process in three parts: see a model of success, name it in concrete steps, and do what it takes to make it real. See It. Name It. Do It.

> ## Core Idea
> The fastest way to develop a skill is to see it, name it, and do it.
> Then repeat until you've mastered it.

If I had not seen Miguel prepare the meal, I wouldn't have captured the subtleties that made his preparation magical. Then I needed to name those steps, and finally I needed to do it myself. The same was true of Laura's instructional team in the vignettes that opened this chapter. Before they could launch the year, Laura had to model the actions of the morning routine for her staff and make sure they could name them so that they'd know what to do when they practiced (See It and Name It). Then they had to rehearse the first day of school (Do It) before they could welcome their students on the real first day of school. Similarly, in their weekly data meetings, they had to see the success and also name the gaps in their students' reading (See It and Name It) before they could make a plan to close those gaps (Do It). See It. Name It. Do It.

We recognize this need in other professions—we'd never ask an aspiring doctor to perform an operation before seeing one in action, or a firefighter to rush to the scene of an emergency without having rehearsed the steps of getting there quickly and prepared. *Leverage Leadership 2.0* simply brings those same principles to education. See It, Name It, and Do It are the three essential steps to implementing any one of the seven levers of school leadership: *seeing* a model of excellence in clear detail; *naming* the qualifying characteristics that make that model effective (so that others can name it as well); and *doing* those actions repeatedly—first behind the scenes in extensive practice sessions, and then daily in the classroom.

Leverage Leadership 2.0 and this guide for principal managers are built on the premise that we need a guide to lock down the same certainty of success that we can find on high-quality teams in any other profession. Our students deserve no less.

HOW TO LIFT THE LEVERS

With this framework in mind, how do principals bring it to life to run their school effectively—and what are the first steps a principal manager can take to prepare them to do so?

Learn the Levers

Learning how to take the lead on each of the seven levers is the first step to locking in a principal's success. Principals and principal managers alike have found that they need to know the levers inside and out, for the benefit not only of themselves but also of the others they lead. If you don't know the lever, you can't lead it or coach it. *Leverage Leadership 2.0* includes not only a detailed chapter on each lever of leadership but also complete sets of workshop materials that can be used to train leaders in the art of each.

Build a Weekly Schedule

Knowing *what* you should be spending time on doesn't do you much good unless you know *when* you're going to do it. Therefore, a weekly schedule that locks in time to be spent on each lever is the right arm of any successful school leader. *Leverage Leadership 2.0* includes a step-by-step guide to building such a schedule. Here's an example of what that schedule looks like when complete.

Eric Diamon's Schedule: Everything

Time	Monday	Tuesday	Wednesday	Thursday	Friday
6 AM					
:30					
7 AM	Breakfast and Morning Circle	Staff Culture Check	Breakfast and Morning Circle	Breakfast and Morning Circle	Greeting and Breakfast
:30					
8 AM	Observe Marcellus, Amanda, Leonard				
:30				Observe Angela	Big-Project Work Time
9 AM	Meet Marcellus		Leadership Team Meeting	Meet Tomas	
:30					
10 AM	Observe Kathryn, Julia, Jessica	Meet Kathryn			
:30		Meet Julia	Observe Mary, Tomas, Becky	Meet Becky	
11 AM				Meet Angela	
:30	Lunch	Lunch	Lunch		
12 PM	Staff Culture Check		Staff Culture Check		
:30	Meet Amanda				Early Dismissal

Time	Monday	Tuesday	Wednesday	Thursday	Friday
1 PM	Meeting with Principal Manager	Principal PD (1/mo) or All-School Walkthrough			Faculty PD Session
:30			Meet Jessica		
2 PM			Meet Mary		
:30					
3 PM				Staff Culture Check	
:30	Meet Leonard	Dismissal	Dismissal	Dismissal	
4 PM					
:30					
5 PM					
:30					

Build a Monthly Map

Some of the levers require month-by-month maintenance to an even greater degree than weekly scheduling. To that end, highly effective school leaders also use monthly task management tools to stay on top of the key actions they need to take at certain times of year. Here's a sample of what two months of a leader's "monthly map" might look like.

Principal Monthly Map

On My Radar

Month	Task
September	1—Launch reading intervention/guided reading. **(Data-Driven Instruction)** 1—Assess curriculum plans for rigor and alignment, and return to teachers. **(Planning)** 2—Hold quarterly leadership team meeting (principal, dean, instructional leaders). **(Leadership Team)**

Month	Task
	3—Videotape planning meetings of all instructional leaders. **(Leadership Team)** 3—Conduct a student and staff culture walkthrough. **(Student Culture, Staff Culture)** 4—Co-observe teachers with instructional leaders. **(Feedback and Observation, Leadership Team)** 4—Set yearly PD goals for all new teachers in observation tracker. **(Feedback and Observation)**
October	1—Design PD session on classroom pacing. **(PD, Student Culture)** 1—Give teachers curriculum planning update and revision time. **(Planning)** 2—Ensure instructional leaders are reviewing video clips with novice teachers. **(Leadership Team)** 3—Administer interim assessment 1. **(Data)** 4—Evaluate school on data-driven instruction rubric. **(Data)** 4—Coordinate grade-level culture walkthroughs. **(Student Culture, Staff Culture)**

Receive Coaching Throughout the Year

With all of this in place, the best way principals can be supported in leveraging leadership is by receiving coaching as they roll the levers out over the course of the year. That's where the principal manager comes in—and that's what the rest of this book covers!

CONCLUSION

Laura Garza achieved phenomenal success at Blanton Elementary School, but she's not alone. Many of her peers in Dallas are also making significant strides because they share a common framework and common coaching, and they have focused on what matters most.

Taking these results to scale is just like leading a symphony—they require a conductor to lead.

Let's dive into how you can be that conductor to create moving music in each of your schools.

Chapter 2

Identifying the Right Action Steps

What Do I Coach?

Walk around with network superintendent Jeanine Zitta from St. Louis Public Schools, and you won't step inside in the central office very often. Instead, you'll find yourself in schools, working alongside a principal.

On this day, Jeanine and her principal Angela Glass are seated at the round table in Angela's office. On the bulletin board behind them you can see the school's values written on colorful construction paper, putting words to the qualities that make the school so vibrant.

Jeanine has just finished praising Angela for the improvements in her feedback meetings, and now they are beginning work on her next stage of development.

"Today I want to dive into the Do It of your feedback meeting," shares Jeanine, "specifically the part 'plan before you practice.' What are the main components of that segment?"

"So, making sure the teacher has any lesson material that they need," Angela comments (Jeanine nods), "and also making sure that they think through and script out what they are going to do in the lesson."

"Yes. So what is the purpose of giving the teacher time to plan before taking it live?" asks Jeanine.

"I find that in the past if I did not give the teacher time to plan," responds Angela, "they'll start practicing and you'll have to stop them, versus getting it right first and then starting the practice."

"Agreed," affirms Jeanine. "I'm going to model the 'plan before practice' segment for you. I'll be you, and you'll be Mr. Mitchell [one of her teachers], and I want you to notice the key leader moves that I make." "OK!" Angela says.

Then Jeanine launches fully into role play, playing the role of Angela. "Mr. Mitchell, so your action step is to redirect students using the least invasive strategy. Using nonverbal cues is the new part of this strategy for you. Let's plan our practice . . ."

Over the course of the next five minutes, Jeanine models how to get the teacher to plan effectively during a feedback meeting, and Angela immediately notices the gap between her own feedback and Jeanine's model. "This change will take me to the next level of rigor and help the teaching get better. I can see if they understand and make the practice tighter."

"Exactly," concurs Jeanine. "Let's plan your next meeting . . ."

 WATCH Clip 1: Zitta—See It and Name It—Manager Feedback Meeting

St. Louis Public Schools is Jeanine Zitta's home. She's worked there for eighteen years, beginning as a teacher before coming into her own as a school leader. Today, Jeanine manages a network of her city's elementary schools—and those schools are taking off. For schools that had been mired in mediocrity, student learning is changing. Of the ten schools that Jeanine has managed for two complete years, every single one of them has improved in both ELA and math (see Figure 2.1). These scores represent the highest growth in the district.

For anyone who has been a principal manager, you know that batting ten for ten in improved scores is nearly unheard of. The secret to Jeanine's success? Following the leader—not herself, but the strongest of the principals she coaches.

"If you manage it correctly, someone else's success can make everyone ask, 'How can I be like that person?'" Jeanine notes wisely. "The highest performers always get the question: 'How did you do that?' but we don't always pay attention to the answer."

That was the hard part for Jeanine in improving her schools: not determining what the challenges were, but naming what action the principals should take that would most effectively address those challenges. The "what to do" was harder than the "what to fix."

Figure 2.1   Missouri State Assessment: St. Louis Network 3 Schools, Percentage at or Above Proficiency in ELA (top) and Math (bottom)

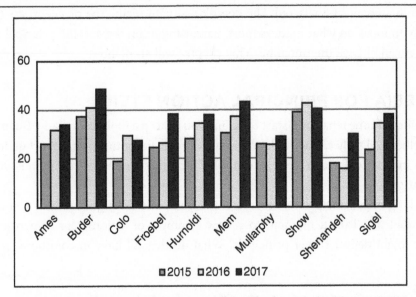

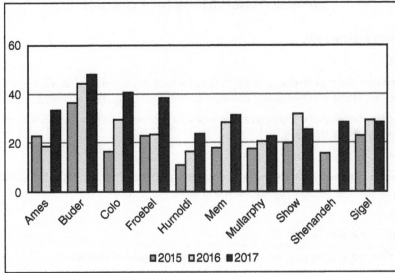

Core Idea

The key to improving school leaders is not only finding what to fix but also naming how to do so.

Determining how to fix something becomes more complicated for a principal manager, as the number of things that can go wrong in a school becomes so large! Yet Jeanine remains undeterred. She doesn't rest with seeing the problem: she finds a pathway to focus on what matters most, narrowing in on the specific principal action step that can change the outcome. This chapter will show how.

CRITERIA FOR PRINCIPAL ACTION STEPS

Any guide to home repair will start by telling you to keep a toolbox on hand. But not just any toolbox will suffice. The guide will also give you a list of the most important tools to include in your toolbox so that you can solve the largest and most common issues that could arise.

Working with principals is no different: if you build the right toolbox, you can fix more problems. Take a moment to review a sample of action steps a manager like Jeanine might deliver to her principals. What do they all have in common?

Sample Action Steps for Principals

Data-Driven Instruction

8. **See It:**
   - Start with the standard(s): unpack the key parts of the standard that align to the student error to ID the most essential conceptual understandings that students must master.
   - Unpack the teacher and student exemplars (or rubrics) to ID how the work demonstrates mastery of the standard.

9. **Name It:**
   - Punch it: succinctly restate the key procedural errors and conceptual misunderstandings, then have the teacher repeat them and write them down.

10. **Do It:**
    - Perfect the plan before you practice.
      - Plan the structure of the reteach: modeling or guided discourse.
      - ID the steps, student materials, and students to monitor.
      - Predict the gap: anticipate likely errors in execution, and practice that part of the meeting.
    - Practice the gap.
      - ID the most essential elements of the reteach for the teacher to practice, especially the parts that will be hardest to master.

- o Prompt the teacher to "go live" and practice the prompts that will be used during the reteach.
- Build an effective follow-up plan.
  - o ID when to teach, when to reassess, and when to revisit this data.
  - o Embed the action plan into upcoming lessons and unit plans.
  - o ID when observations will take place to see plan in action and how it will be assessed.

Stop and Jot

Sample Action Steps for Principals

What characteristics do these action steps have in common? Write your response here.

_____

_____

_____

_____

_____

These sorts of action steps are the pinnacle of simplicity: they are focused, targeted, and self-explanatory. And if you notice a striking similarity in the characteristics of these action steps to the characteristics of action steps we recommend for teachers in *Leverage Leadership 2.0,* you are right. They are not book-size but bite-size. Just like teachers, leaders grow most quickly when their managers narrow their focus to the highest-leverage action step.

Core Idea

The smaller and more precise the action step, the quicker the growth.
Be bite-size, not book-size.

The power of bite-size action steps is well chronicled by Daniel Coyle in *The Talent Code* [1] and by *Leverage Leadership 2.0*: when you focus only on what matters most, you build the right foundation, which accelerates sustainable growth of a person's expertise. If it works for students, athletes, musicians, and teachers, it certainly works for principals as well!

The criteria for an excellent principal action step are the same as those for a teacher action step:

- **Highest leverage.** Will this help the leader develop most quickly and effectively? Is it connected to a larger PD goal?

- **Measurable.** The action step is what the leader can practice: it names the "what" (e.g., See It—start with the standard) and the "how" (e.g., fully unpack the standard to identify what a student must know and do to be able to master the standard).

- **Bite-size.** If your principal can't make the change in a week, the action step isn't small enough!

Keys to Great Action Steps

Great action steps are:

- **Highest leverage.** Will this help the leader develop most quickly and effectively? Is it connected to a larger PD goal?

- **Measurable.** The action step is what the leader can practice: it names the "what" and the "how."

- **Bite-size.** If your leader can't make the change in a week, the action step isn't small enough!

Although the criteria for effective principal action steps are universally applicable, what makes action steps for principals more challenging is the number of layers. Let's consider why that's the case.

When Jeanine walks around a school with a principal to observe, she will notice the strengths and areas of growth for each teacher. Her first actions will be to determine what the teachers need to do to improve—a teacher-facing action step. At the same time, though, she needs to determine where the gap is in the principal's leadership that is keeping the teachers from getting better faster. As a result, she often ends up generating both a teacher action step *and* a principal action step. That's complex—and it's one reason why, before we train our eyes, we often forget to identify action steps for our principals as well as our teachers.

To make it easier to see the right principal action steps clearly, we have studied the action steps that top principal managers give to their principals, and we've consolidated them into one document, organized by leadership lever. The full document, the Leverage Leadership Sequence of Action Steps for Principals, can be found at the end of this chapter and in the DVD. Here is one lever—observation and feedback—as an example. What do you notice about how the action steps are organized?

Leverage Leadership Sequence of Action Steps for Principals

Observation and Feedback

LEVER	KEY ACTIONS IN SEQUENCE
	PLAN
OBSERVATION AND FEEDBACK	1. **Build weekly observation schedule for yourself and other instructional leaders/coaches:** • Establish and maintain own observation schedule and Observation Tracker. • Establish observation schedules and trackers for leadership team to effectively distribute observation of all teachers. • Adjust the schedule as needed to address trends and/or support struggling teachers. 2. **Prepare:** Stick to an exemplar script (See It, Name It, Do It feedback protocol) to ensure that your prompts are clear, economical, and aimed at the highest-leverage action step.
	EXECUTE

	Action Steps
	3. **ID highest-leverage school-wide and individual teacher action steps:**
	• Use your tools (Get Better Faster Scope and Sequence, student data) to create action steps that are
	  o Highest leverage (will student achievement improve tomorrow as a result of this action step?)
	  o Measurable and bite-size

LEVER	KEY ACTIONS IN SEQUENCE
	EXECUTE

Effective Feedback Meetings

4. **See It—see the success:**

- Prepare and deliver precise, authentic praise rooted in previous action step(s).

- Ask teacher to describe the impact: "What has been the impact of this on your classroom?"

5. **See It—show a model and see the gap:**

- Show a model—video, live model, script, lesson plan—that highlights key actions for the teacher.

- Fully unpack to ID the model: start with the end in mind and ask precise questions to identify all key actions (e.g., "What is the purpose of . . .?" "What did she do next?").

- Ask "What is the gap between what you just saw and what you did?"

6. **Do It—perfect the plan before you practice:**

- Give your teacher time to script out her actions before you start the practice and between rounds of practice.

- Revise the script until it is perfect.

- Use an exemplar to perfect the plan.

7. **Do It—practice the gap:**

- Practice at the point of error: anticipate what teachers or students could do/say incorrectly during the practice and plan for those mistakes.

- Practice the gap: set up practice so that the teacher practices the actions that are most critical for the action step.

8. **Do It—practice. Go from simple to more complex:**

- Practice with upcoming lessons/meetings to apply the skill to multiple scenarios.

- Start with simple practice; when teacher masters it, add complexity (student wrong answers or noncompliance).

- Narrow the practice to repeat it more times and get more at-bats.

- Stop the practice, provide real-time feedback, and redo.

(Vertical label at left: OBSERVATION AND FEEDBACK)

LEVER	KEY ACTIONS IN SEQUENCE

9. Name It—punch it:

- Punch the action step by naming the "what" and the "how" clearly and concisely.

- Be bite-size, not book-size: limit the action steps to what the teacher can master in a week.

- Have teacher write it down and check for understanding to make sure she has it.

MONITOR AND FOLLOW UP

10. Do It—follow up. Articulate clear next steps:

- Set dates: all deliverables have clear timelines and are written into both the leader's and teacher's calendar.

- Establish follow-up and (when applicable) real-time feedback cues to be used during the observation.

11. Provide real-time feedback:

- Choose highest-leverage moments for real-time classroom feedback.

- Use least invasive method for real-time feedback that is appropriate for the teacher.
    - Silent signal
    - Whisper prompt:
        - Name what to do
        - State the rationale
        - State what you'll look for/how you will support
        - (All in 45 seconds max)
    - Verbal prompt/model
    - Extended model

(side label) OBSERVATION AND FEEDBACK

Right from the beginning, you probably noticed an overall structure: plan, execute, monitor. This same organization exists for all the leadership levers. (Some, such as student culture, will add an additional section for rollout, where what you do in the first weeks at the start of school will be distinct from the rest of the year.)

Why use this structure? Imagine you are working with a principal on improving her observation and feedback. You ask her to film one of her feedback meetings, and you note that it is mediocre across the board. Where would you start guiding the principal to improve? You could start by trying to fix the quality of her prompts: getting the teacher to do more of the thinking. But even better would be to start from the first section: plan. If the leader doesn't have a schedule of regular observations and feedback, then fixing the issues of the feedback meeting won't help, because few teachers will be getting feedback in the first place! Here we see the power of the organization of the action steps: always get the plan right before you focus on the execution. Once the plan is in place, you can see where the breakdown occurred in the execution or monitoring.

Core Idea

To get the execution right, you need to get your plan right.
Plan. Roll out. Execute. Monitor.

These principal action steps were not created in a vacuum or a think tank: they were developed by observing thousands of hours of footage of principals in action as well as managers meeting with their principals. We noticed that the highest-achieving managers—the ones who got the largest number of their schools to succeed—had much more precise action steps, and they followed a sequence. What we've done here is put them all in one place for you to use.

HOW TO USE THE LEVERAGE LEADERSHIP SEQUENCE OF ACTION STEPS FOR PRINCIPALS

Think about the power of using these principal action steps. Rather than working with a blank slate trying to spot the problem a principal is having, you have a starting point—a guide amid all the noise of trying to see a principal in action.

Here are a few key tips that will help increase the impact of the Leverage Leadership Sequence of Action Steps for Principals on your daily practice:

- **Start the year with culture.** If you get student culture right in the first months, you tee up the year to succeed. If you don't, you will struggle against it all year. Even seasoned veterans benefit from starting the year with a focus on culture. Focusing on the plan and rollout of student culture systems will pay long-term dividends.

- **Focus first on the super-levers.** Student culture isn't the only super-lever: data-driven instruction is just as essential. Without it, you won't be able to shift the focus from the teaching to the learning. Your principal might have lots of other areas to work on, but start with the two super-levers first!

- **Keep it narrow.** It might be tempting to work with a principal on three or four leadership levers at a time. He or she will certainly be working in multiple areas from the sequence of action steps at once: staff culture gatherings, PD, curriculum planning, leadership teams, and so forth. Nonetheless, narrowing *your* focus will have a greater impact on the principal's work than spreading it across multiple topics. It is far better for you to perfect one part of a principal's leadership (e.g., weekly data meetings) than to dabble in all seven levers. Remember, the sharper and more precise your focus, the quicker the growth, because you build a foundation that will stick.

CASE STUDIES—TRY IT YOURSELF

In order to get used to this framework, let's try it! What follows are four case studies of actual principals whom I have observed and coached. After reading each case study, pull out the Leverage Leadership Sequence of Action Steps for Principals at the end of the chapter (or print out the whole sequence in printer-friendly formatting from the DVD), and determine what action step you would give to each principal.

Case Study 1: Student Culture

Principal Case Study 1
Student Culture

Context

Today is the beginning of teacher orientation the week before school starts, and your principal is rolling out his vision for student culture. You spent a lot of time with him over the summer defining the vision (principal action step 1) and developing a minute-by-minute plan for student culture during the whole school day (action steps 2 and 3). One of the particular areas you and your principal wanted to improve was the launch of the school day and of every class period. Last year, the school didn't have a clearly defined entry procedure, which led to a chaotic start to each class, contributing to lots of off-task behavior and minimally productive lessons. As you created the plan for orientation, the two of you decided to focus one of the first sessions on classroom entry: how to begin the lesson effectively in each class period. You developed a workshop agenda following the exemplar of the Student Culture workshop from *Leverage Leadership 2.0*: you planned a hook, a model of classroom entry, and time for the staff to practice and rehearse (action step 4). Now you are observing your principal as he leads this workshop with his staff.

Observation of Student Culture Rollout

The principal starts with a nice hook: a video clip from the movie *Drumline* that has the teachers smiling and talking about the power of being "one sound." Then the leader begins his model of an opening routine. The principal was a very effective teacher himself, with strong presence that had students always engaged. He goes into his natural "teacher voice" and leads the entry routine. Teachers are highly engaged as they watch him model shaking students' hands, commenting differently to each student, and using his charisma to set the expectation for a strong class literally from the door.

After his model, the principal breaks the teachers into groups so that they can practice the entry routine themselves. As the practice begins, many of the teachers try to be like the principal with their tone of voice and charisma, but it isn't nearly as powerful. They start making comments to each student, but they don't have the same impact. You can already see that a number of teachers are not going to have as effective an entry routine as the one the principal modeled. The principal floats around watching the practice, but he doesn't jump in. He offers a few words of encouragement as the practice continues.

When you debrief afterward, the principal says that he noticed that the practice wasn't as effective as his model, but he didn't know what to do to improve it.

Answer: When Jeanine leads a rehearsal or practice that doesn't go as well as she hoped, she makes sure to begin with a root-cause analysis. A number of factors can contribute to ineffective practice. Was it the principal's lack of real-time coaching during the practice? Was it the directions on what they should be practicing? Or was it rooted in the quality of the model that the teachers are trying to emulate? We don't know all the details in this abbreviated case study, but with the information provided, there is one action step that will likely be most impactful:

- Model: exaggerate the model to reinforce every action you want to see.
  - Exaggerate your body language and tone to give them a precise model that they can follow: lean more when scanning the room, narrate the positive, and punch your directions with a strong voice.

Often, when principals who were once strong classroom teachers try to model for their staff, they rely on how they would have done the action, forgetting to model all the small actions that make the difference in getting students to follow. Once you are a master teacher, you can simply say, "You may now start your writing," and everyone will follow. But for a new teacher, that won't work. Therefore, one of the most common action steps I give to leaders when modeling is to exaggerate their model. Make sure you're modeling not what you yourself would do naturally but what will work for teachers who don't already know how to do what you're showing them. This often means exaggerating body language (e.g., standing up taller than you would normally, tilting your shoulders more, and rising on your tiptoes to show that you are scanning the room); modulating your voice more (e.g., give it a more exaggerated formal tone); and tightening your words (e.g., add the type of positive narration or quick correction that you would have to do if not every student followed you immediately). Another way to think about it is that you need to bring your "B game," during which you need to follow every step of a process, rather than your "A game," during which you can simply give directions and everything will work perfectly.

Core Idea

When you model, bring your "B game," not your "A game":
model what a new teacher will need to do, rather than what you'd do naturally.

Case Study 2: Data-Driven Instruction

Principal Case Study 2

Data-Driven Instruction

Context

You are working with your principal around data-driven instruction to set the foundation for effective teaching and student learning. In the past months, you have locked in the action steps in the Plan section of data-driven instruction: you have already worked on establishing an effective yearly calendar with interim assessments (principal action step 1), quality curriculum (action step 2), structures for data meetings and monitoring tools (3 and 4). You have also rolled out PD on data-driven instruction (5) and identified the key trends in student learning (6). With these actions established, you go to observe and take notes on the principal's regularly scheduled weekly data meetings with the fourth-grade team of three teachers.

Observation of Weekly Data Meeting

The group seems pretty jovial, and there is good energy as they review student work. You can see that this is not the first time they've had a data meeting. Your leader is following the *Leverage Leadership 2.0* Weekly Data Meeting one-pager, and you see them start by working through one of the challenging standards from the last interim assessment. They unpack the standard and the teacher exemplar—but it takes them a fairly long time because they go around multiple times to add more answers. Then they look at imperfect student work and find a common pattern to the error: the students don't understand how the value of the denominator determines the size of the parts in the numerator. After they reach that conclusion, the leader gives each of them a few minutes to plan a reteach lesson to close the gap, and then she asks one to stand up and try it. The teacher jumps into modeling how to do these fraction problems, and you notice that it is not a very effective reteach plan. Your principal notices the same thing and pretty quickly interrupts the teacher and starts giving a lot of real-time feedback to fix the errors. After each piece of feedback, the teacher tries again, and then they fix another part of it. They haven't been able to completely fix the reteach lesson when time runs out and the teachers head back to class.

Stop and Jot

Case Study 2

Review the Data-Driven Instruction section of the Leverage Leadership Sequence of Action Steps for Principals. What action step would you give this principal?

_____

_____

_____

Answer: There are clearly many strengths to this meeting: an obvious continuity (i.e., this is not a one-time meeting), and good understanding of the standard and unpacking the gap. Yet there are a number of areas for growth where you could focus in this meeting. The meeting doesn't seem to be run very efficiently, which leads to them running out of time to fully practice their reteach lesson for next year. They spend more time than they need to at the beginning looking at the standard, and they spend a lot of time trying to fix the reteach plan during the teacher's role play of the practice.

So what is the action step that will make the biggest difference in the bottom line: a better reteach plan that will improve student learning? Although moving more quickly through the standard would help, that won't fix the root cause: the initial reteach plan that the teacher developed was not very strong. No matter how much more efficiently the leader ran the first part of the meeting, that wouldn't help improve the quality of the reteach plan. The trouble was that although the leader astutely noticed the problems with the reteach and tried to fix them during the practice, the result of waiting until the live practice to do so was that all the teacher experienced was reteaching incorrectly. Therefore, our recommendation for highest-leverage action step would be:

- Perfect the plan before you practice.
    - Spar with an exemplar reteach plan: put the two reteach plans side by side and make revisions right into the teacher's script.
    - Don't begin to practice the reteach until you have perfected the plan.

Think about the impact of this action step. Although many other action steps will improve the meeting, this one will most quickly affect the quality of implementation of the reteach plan, because having the right plan in place will enable the teacher to practice effectively—as opposed to imperfectly. That's the kind of practice that will translate into effective teaching when the moment comes for the teacher to return to the classroom. Perfect the plan, and you perfect the teaching.

> ## Core Idea
> Perfect the plan, and you perfect the teaching.

Case Study 3: Observation and Feedback

Principal Case Study 3
Observation and Feedback

Context

Your principal has effectively established the structures for student culture and data-driven instruction, so you are working with her on the lever of observation and feedback. You already set up a regular observation schedule (principal action step 1), and you have tracked that she and her leadership team are maintaining pretty consistent observations. Your principal films one of her feedback meetings and gives it to you to review the day before you are going to meet.

Observation of Feedback Meeting

As you review the video, you can see evidence that your principal is using the See It, Name It, Do It protocol with her teacher. She starts by focusing on how to run small-group stations in his classroom.

"I'm going to model for you what it looks like," she says. "For example, I would first make sure that everyone is listening to me. Then I would say something like 'We're about to transition to small-group stations.' After saying that, I would describe what's going to happen in each group, something like 'Group 1 will be working on a vocabulary game: using the dictionary to determine the meaning of new words. Each student has to write down the definitions for five new vocabulary words.' Then I would explain each other station. Then after describing each station, I would state the general rules: only one station at a time, restaurant-level voices, and write your answers down. Does that make sense? So . . . based on that model, what are the important things for you to do when setting up your small-group station work?"

The teacher enthusiastically nods and identifies that the specificity of these instructions gives the students clarity about what they should do. The principal then names the teacher's action step: deliver explicit instructions for group work with clear roles for each person. The teacher nods and writes down the action step for himself. The leader gives him a few minutes to write down his instructions for the upcoming activity that afternoon, and then he talks through them with the principal, similarly to how the principal modeled. They end the meeting, and the teacher states that he is excited to try this out.

The next day you meet with the principal and go to observe the teacher. You notice that as the teacher gives the first instructions for the opening Do Now (independent brief writing activity), he delivers them softly and tentatively, and about a third of the students don't pay attention and don't begin writing. The teacher then reminds the students quietly ("Some people aren't writing yet; everyone should be writing"), and a few of those students start working. This continues throughout the class, with slightly more students going off-task with each new activity. When it gets to small-group station time, about half the students are not paying attention, and the teacher has the same struggle when delivering the directions. Although he's using the script he prepared in the feedback meeting, the classroom quickly devolves into a scene of a large amount of unorganized activity.

Stop and Jot

Case Study 3

Review the Observation and Feedback section of your Leverage Leadership Sequence of Action Steps for Principals. What action step would you give this principal?

_____

_____

_____

Answer: As we observe this leader, many areas come to the surface, and the bottom line is that teaching does not improve. The core question here is, What is the root cause of the problem?

We see that the leader doesn't do a real model for the teacher: she just talks her way through what she would do. Because of that, the teacher never sees what the model would look and sound like when being fully delivered to the students. The errors continue in the practice when the teacher doesn't fully practice as he would in his classroom; saying "What I would do is . . ." is not the same as authentic practice. So the teacher hasn't fully practiced an effective model before teaching.

One could certainly argue that the leader should have given a better model (e.g., exaggerate your model, as we mentioned Case Study 1), or that she and her teacher should perfect the plan before practice (as in Case Study 2). But either of these might still leave the teacher floundering. The root problem wasn't small-group stations in and of themselves; it was the teacher's inability to deliver instructions with authority. Because that wasn't the action step the principal focused on, the teacher didn't practice the true gap in his instruction: *how* to deliver instructions, not what to say. Thus our recommendation for highest-leverage action step would be:

- Identify the highest-leverage school-wide and individual teacher action step:
  - Utilize your Get Better Faster Scope and Sequence to select the highest-leverage action step: start from the top of the sequence and stop at the first major gap.
  - For this teacher, the action step could be Strong Voice: stand and speak with purpose:
    - Square Up, Stand Still: when giving instructions, stop moving and strike a formal pose.
    - Formal register: use formal register, including tone and word choice.

To be clear, the leader will still struggle if she doesn't improve the quality of her model, but if she's not focused on what matters most for that teacher's development, improving the model won't make the necessary impact.

CONCLUSION

It may seem counterintuitive at first, but Jeanine says she doubts her skill as a leader most when she works with her strongest principal. "I always think, 'What can I do? She's a god,'" Jeanine says, laughing. But what Jeanine does, ultimately, is what makes her successful. She codifies what the strongest principal is doing so that she can coach the others to do the same, and then she uses the principal action steps to identify feedback even her most advanced school leader can grow from. And the feedback Jeanine receives tells her that this is working: this principal she admires so much has told her, "I get better faster with you coaching me."

If you've felt uncertain of your own ability to guide your principals, know that you are not alone! Concerns like these are the very reason the Leverage Leadership Sequence of Action Steps for Principals pages that follow are so useful. They give you more than just a list of action steps: they give you focus. They enable you to shut out the din of everything school leadership entails and focus on what matters most: the levers that drive achievement.

We've now presented the "what" (clear action steps for principals). The next chapters will focus on "how": how we coach for success.

Leverage Leadership Sequence of Action Steps for Principal

Lever	Key Actions in Sequence
	Plan
Data-Driven Instruction	**Assessments and Curriculum—Align the Rigor** 1. **Lock in quality interim assessments:** • ID the end-goal assessment (state test, college entrance exam, college assessment) that exemplifies what successful students should know and be able to do. • ID essential content and rigor that students must master for success on end-goal assessment. • Acquire or develop effective interim assessments (IAs) that are aligned to end-goal assessments. • Develop a common IA calendar that identifies when IAs will take place, who and what will be assessed, and when IA data analysis meetings will take place.

LEVER	KEY ACTIONS IN SEQUENCE
	PLAN

<table>
<tr><td rowspan="1" style="writing-mode:vertical-lr">DATA-DRIVEN INSTRUCTION</td><td>

2. **Lock in high-quality lesson plans and curriculum materials that align to the assessments:**
   - See Planning section for details.

Data Meetings—Tools and Structures for Weekly Data/IA Meetings

3. **Establish essential data meeting structures that result in evidence-based action planning:**
   - Create meeting schedule to conduct data meetings to analyze IA data (every 6 weeks) and to conduct weekly data meetings (WDMs).
   - Establish consistent protocols and prework expectations for effective analysis meetings (e.g., IA analysis meeting protocol, WDM analysis protocol).
   - Develop a system to regularly collect high, medium, and low samples of student work (e.g., Exit Tickets, spiral review) to use as evidence to ID trends in student learning.

4. **Create effective principal monitoring tools for all post-assessment action plans, including:**
   - Develop an action plan tracker that identifies teacher reteach goals, timeline, and focus area.
   - Create systems to have access to assessments and/or DDI action plan when observing.
   - Create observation schedules to observe teachers in reteaching implementation.

</td></tr>
</table>

| | **ROLL OUT** |

PD on Data-Driven Instruction (DDI)

5. **Roll out PD for data-driven instruction:**
   - Plan and roll out PD on DDI, the power of the question, and writing exemplars.
   - Develop and roll out exemplar IA analysis to set clear expectations for teacher analysis.

Lever	Key Actions in Sequence

	Roll Out
	• Create repeated opportunities during PD to practice analyzing student data/work and creating 6-week action plans (IAs) or targeted reteach plans (WDM).

	Execute

Data-Driven Instruction

Analyze for Trends

6. **Conduct a deep analysis of the data to ID school-wide and teacher-specific trends:**

   • Find the overall trend.

     o For IAs: ID school-wide patterns in the data: outlier teachers and students (low and high) and key standards that need focus.

     o For WDMs: review the student work to select the highest-leverage standards or question to focus on for analysis.

   • ID the key conceptual understanding and error for a given standard or task.

     o Determine what students should be able to do and say to demonstrate mastery of the standard or task.

     o ID the key gap between the ideal response and student work: both the key procedural errors and conceptual misunderstandings.

     o Determine the highest-leverage action steps to take to close the gap.

Data Meetings—Lead Effective Weekly Data and IA Analysis Meetings with Teachers

7. **Prepare:**

   • Narrow your focus: pick the assessment item and student work in advance that highlight key errors.

   • Prepare the exemplar and write your meeting script to ensure an effective, efficient meeting.

8. **See It:**

   • Start with the standard(s): unpack the key parts of the standard that align to the student error to ID the most essential conceptual understandings that students must master.

LEVER	KEY ACTIONS IN SEQUENCE
	EXECUTE

- Unpack the teacher and student exemplars (or rubrics) to ID how the work demonstrates mastery of the standard.

9. **Name It:**
   - Punch it: succinctly restate the key procedural errors and conceptual misunderstandings, then have the teacher repeat them and write them down.

10. **Do It:**
    - Perfect the plan before you practice.
      - Plan the structure of the reteach: modeling or guided discourse.
      - ID the steps, student materials, and students to monitor.
      - Predict the gap: anticipate likely errors in execution and practice that part of the meeting.
    - Practice the gap.
      - ID the most essential elements of the reteach for the teacher to practice, especially the parts that will be hardest to master.
      - Prompt the teacher to "go live" and practice the prompts that will be used during the reteach.
    - Build an effective follow-up plan.
      - ID when to teach, when to reassess, and when to revisit this data.
      - Embed the action plan into upcoming lessons and unit plans.
      - ID when observations will take place to see plan in action and how it will be assessed.

	MONITOR AND FOLLOW UP

11. **Actively monitor implementation of action plans:**
    - Observe the reteach.
      - Start from the exemplar teacher and observe same-subject teachers back-to-back.

(Left vertical label: DATA-DRIVEN INSTRUCTION)

LEVER	KEY ACTIONS IN SEQUENCE
	MONITOR AND FOLLOW UP

- o ID the gap between the exemplar teacher and other teachers.
- o ID the gap between the original plan and execution and between student work and exemplar.
- Observe weekly data meetings (WDMs) of other instructional leaders (live or via video).
  - o ID the patterns across meetings and the key areas of growth for the leader's facilitation.
- Track implementation of 6-week action plans and student outcomes following reteach.
  - o Have teacher post lesson plans and/or 6-week action plans in the classroom to be able to observe both the plan and the execution to ID gaps.
- Create system for teacher teams to collect student work between WDMs.

12. **Monitor student work in each class using a sequence:**
    - (A) pen-to-paper, (B) annotations/strategies, and (C) right answers

LEVER	KEY ACTIONS IN SEQUENCE
	PLAN

STUDENT CULTURE

Set the Vision

1. **Define your vision for student culture:**
   - See a model.
     - o Review videos of implementation (e.g., from *Get Better Faster, Leverage Leadership, Teach Like a Champion*) and/or visit high-performing schools or classrooms.
     - o Record what teachers, leaders, and students say and do.
   - Define the model for your own school's routines and procedures.
     - o Write what the leaders, teachers, and students should be doing.

Identifying the Right Action Steps   49

Lever	Key Actions in Sequence
	PLAN

STUDENT CULTURE

- o Enumerate what will happen if a student doesn't follow directions.
- o Create a school-wide culture rubric that defines the following:
  - Common language that teachers and leaders will use
  - Vision for all school-wide and classroom routines and systems
- Anticipate the gap.
  - o Determine what it would look like if student culture was executed poorly.
  - o What would ineffective leaders and teachers be doing?
  - o What would the students be doing if it was implemented poorly?

2. **Name It—build a minute-by-minute plan for every routine, procedure, and all-school culture moment:**
- Craft minute-by-minute systems for routines and procedures.
  - o Name what leaders, students, and teachers will do in a comprehensive, sequential, minute-by-minute plan.
    - Describe every part of the day: arrival/breakfast, hallway transitions, in-class routines (including first and last 5 min of class), lunch, dismissal.
    - Include what will happen when students do not follow directions.
- Set goals and deadlines.
  - o Set a concrete, measurable goal—e.g., hallway transitions will reduce to 1 min; increase all hands raised to 100%.
  - o ID when the system will be *introduced* and when the goal will be *met*.
  - o Determine the tool for measurement (e.g., Student Culture Rubric).

LEVER	KEY ACTIONS IN SEQUENCE

	PLAN

3. Name It—build systems to manage student discipline (asst. principal, dean of students, etc.):

- Set up effective systems and routines for the leader who will drive student culture.

- Set a weekly and daily schedule for that leader.

- Create a clear protocol for responding to specific student discipline situations.

- Build a standing agenda for principal–culture leader check-ins that includes:

  o Data review of student discipline issues and most pressing student issues

  o Feedback to the leader and to teachers who need support

  o Review of send-out or suspension data to problem-solve ways to prevent the behavior

	ROLL OUT

STUDENT CULTURE

4. Plan the rollout/rehearsal:

- Plan the rollout.

  o Script a hook:

    ▪ Frontload school values/mission—short and sweet speech that states rationale and purpose.

  o Script the model.

    ▪ Using clear and concise language, tell them the procedure and the sequence of the procedure. Everyone needs to know what it will look like.

    ▪ Script what you will narrate as you model to highlight key takeaways.

  o Plan the staff practice of the routine/procedure.

    ▪ Script what you will say and do and script what teachers will say and do (roles, timing, etc.).

    ▪ Script what real-time feedback you will give during practice, with associated prompts.

Lever	Key Actions in Sequence
	Roll Out

5. Roll out/rehearse:

- See It—model the routine/procedure.
  - o Hook: deliver a hook (short and sweet) that gives them the "why."
  - o Frame: name what you want them to observe: "As you watch the model of [routine/procedure], I want you to be thinking about . . ."
  - o Model: exaggerate the model to reinforce every action you want to see.
- Name It—debrief the model.
  - o Ask "What did you notice? Teacher actions? Student actions?"
  - o Narrate the why: "Why is that [action] important?"
  - o Reflect: "Jot down your key takeaways before we jump into practice."
- Do It—practice the routine/procedure.
  - o Give clear What to Do directions:
    - What the main participant will do (time for her to plan/script her actions)
    - What the audience will do (cue cards, preprepared student roles)
  - o Round 1—practice the basic routine and procedure from start to finish.
    - Give feedback at the point of error and have them do it again.
  - o Round 2 (after teachers have built muscle memory)—add complexity (e.g., student misbehavior, student learning errors).
  - o Lock it in and rename the action plan:
    - "How did what we practice meet or enhance the action plan we named?"

(vertical label in left column: STUDENT CULTURE)

LEVER	KEY ACTIONS IN SEQUENCE
	EXECUTE

STUDENT CULTURE

6. **Lead publicly:**

- Be present and be seen in key areas (lunch, hallways, struggling classrooms, etc.).
- Communicate urgency (verbal and nonverbal).
  - o Nonverbal: point to students who need redirecting; move students along.
  - o Verbal: Do It Again until 100%; challenge ("First period did this. Can you do it, too?").
- Provide immediate feedback.
  - o Model concrete phrases and actions that teachers should use (keep it succinct).
  - o Address student noncompliance on the spot; follow up face-to-face with teacher.
  - o Use precise praise and celebrate success (individual and team) verbally and via email.

7. **Manage individually:**

- Teachers—have "course correction" conversations when they are struggling.
  - o ID the challenge.
  - o State the impact.
  - o Make bite-size action plan with prompt implementation on a set timeline.
- Leaders—implement check-in with the leader in charge of student discipline issues (AP/dean).
  - o Model effective student de-escalation and reflection techniques for the AP/dean and have AP/dean execute.
  - o Monitor and give AP/dean real-time feedback to ensure AP/dean meets current action step.
- Students—lead effective discipline conversations by following the model.
  - o Listen: ask them to explain their version of what happened.

LEVER	KEY ACTIONS IN SEQUENCE

- o Name the problem and then the consequence.
- o Share why this is important (back to shared mission and long-term dreams for the child).
- o End with shared commitment to work together.
- Families—lead effective discipline conversations with families.
  - o Name the problem and then the consequence.
  - o Listen: acknowledge their feelings and their concerns ("open face," eye contact, emotional constancy).
  - o Economy of language: keep language concise and precise, and stick to the script.

MONITOR AND COURSE-CORRECT

STUDENT CULTURE

8. **Measure student culture and ID the gaps:**
   - Via a school walkthrough, ID students and teachers not implementing routines effectively and ID the action steps.
     - o With Student Culture Rubric in hand, ID where the breakdown occurs:
       - ▪ What student actions or inactions are indicators of the problem?
       - ▪ What teacher actions or inactions are causing the problem?
       - ▪ What leader actions or inactions are causing the problem?
     - o Bring people outside your leadership team to observe your school and ID the big rocks to move your school culture forward.
   - Targeted improvements: choose one row on the Student Culture Rubric and set a specific goal for a score by a specific date. Develop clear action steps and implement. Rescore that row on a regular basis.

LEVER	KEY ACTIONS IN SEQUENCE
	MONITOR AND COURSE-CORRECT
STUDENT CULTURE	9. **Lead a whole-school reset of a specific, high-leverage routine/ procedure:** • Revisit the model: what the routine should look like. • See the gap: have teachers/leaders ID the gaps. • Model the reset (follow the actions in the rollout section). • Execute a daily walkthrough to monitor the targeted action steps. • Communicate to staff the progress and next steps on a daily basis until the goal is met.

LEVER	KEY ACTIONS IN SEQUENCE
	PLAN
OBSERVATION AND FEEDBACK	1. **Build weekly observation schedule for yourself and other instructional leaders/coaches:** • Establish and maintain own observation schedule and observation tracker. • Establish observation schedules and trackers for leadership team to effectively distribute observation of all teachers. • Adjust the schedule as needed to address trends and/or support struggling teachers. 2. **Prepare:** Stick to an exemplar script (See It, Name It, Do It feedback protocol) to ensure that your prompts are clear, economical, and aimed at the highest-leverage action step.
	EXECUTE

	Action Steps
	3. **ID highest-leverage school-wide and individual teacher action steps:**
	• Use your tools (Get Better Faster Scope and Sequence, student data) to create action steps that are
	   o Highest leverage (will student achievement improve tomorrow as a result of this action step?)
	   o Measurable and bite-size

LEVER	KEY ACTIONS IN SEQUENCE
	EXECUTE

Effective Feedback Meetings

4. **See It—see the success:**
   - Prepare and deliver precise, authentic praise rooted in previous action step(s).
   - Ask teacher to describe the impact: "What has been the impact of this on your classroom?"

5. **See It—show a model and see the gap:**
   - Show a model—video, live model, script, lesson plan—that highlights key actions for the teacher.
   - Fully unpack to ID the model: start with the end in mind and ask precise questions to identify all key actions (e.g., What is the purpose of . . . ?" "What did she do next?").
   - Ask "What is the gap between what you just saw and what you did?"

6. **Do It—perfect the plan before you practice:**
   - Give your teacher time to script out her actions before you start the practice and between rounds of practice.
   - Revise the script until it is perfect.
   - Use an exemplar to perfect the plan.

7. **Do It—practice the gap:**
   - Practice at the point of error: anticipate what teachers or students could do/say incorrectly during the practice and plan for those mistakes.
   - Practice the gap: set up practice so that the teacher practices the actions that are most critical for the action step.

8. **Do It—practice. Go from simple to more complex:**
   - Practice with upcoming lessons/meetings to apply the skill to multiple scenarios.
   - Start with simple practice; when teacher masters it, add complexity (student wrong answers or noncompliance).
   - Narrow the practice to repeat it more times and get more at-bats.
   - Stop the practice, provide real-time feedback, and redo.

(Left vertical label: OBSERVATION AND FEEDBACK)

LEVER	KEY ACTIONS IN SEQUENCE
	EXECUTE

9. Name It—punch it:

- Punch the action step by naming the "what" and the "how" clearly and concisely.
- Be bite-size, not book-size: limit the action steps to what the teacher can master in a week.
- Have teacher write it down and check for understanding to make sure she has it.

MONITOR AND FOLLOW UP

10. Do It—follow up. Articulate clear next steps:

- Set dates: all deliverables have clear timelines and are written into both the leader's and teacher's calendar.
- Establish follow-up and (when applicable) real-time feedback cues to be used during the observation.

11. Provide real-time feedback:

- Choose highest-leverage moments for real-time classroom feedback.
- Use least invasive method for real-time feedback that is appropriate for the teacher.
  - o Silent signal
  - o Whisper prompt:
    - Name what to do
    - State the rationale
    - State what you'll look for/how you will support
    - (All in 45 seconds max)
  - o Verbal prompt/model
  - o Extended model

(Left margin, rotated: OBSERVATION AND FEEDBACK)

Lever	Key Actions in Sequence
	Plan
Planning	**Curriculum—Unit Plans Aligned to Assessment**
	1. **Design high-quality unit plans that align to the end-goal assessments:**
	• Define success: ID exemplar unit plans and name the essential components—they are aligned to a college-ready end-goal assessment (see Chapter 1, Data-Driven Instruction, in *Leverage Leadership 2.0*), teach both content and skill, and are memorable.
	• Acquire or design unit plans that include all essential components.
	Lesson Plans
	2. **Plan effective lesson plans:**
	• Define success: ID exemplar lesson plans and name the essential components—data-driven objective, aligned Exit Ticket, adequate time for practice, and effective guided discourse or modeling.
	• Acquire or design lesson plans that include all essential components.
	Planning Tools and Structures
	3. **Establish essential unit and lesson planning structures that result in consistent lesson plan creation:**
	• Establish essential curriculum planning structures and templates for yearlong plans, unit plans, and weekly and daily lesson plans.
	• Establish effective protocols for creation of unit and lesson plans (when plans will be submitted, who will review them, etc.).
	Execute
	Planning Meetings—Lead Effective Planning Meetings with Teachers
	4. **Prepare:**
	• Narrow your focus: pick the lesson or unit that requires the most focus.

Lever	Key Actions in Sequence
Planning	**Execute**
	• Familiarize yourself with the standards, prepare the exemplar, and write your meeting script to ensure an effective meeting. 5. **Map out the week:** • Set the core content for the week: key reteach standards to spiral, routine tasks (e.g., fluency work, labs, etc.). • Set the objectives for each day. 6. **See It:** • Start with the assessment and standard(s): fully unpack the standard to ID the most essential conceptual understandings that students must master. • Write the teacher exemplars and rubric to name what work demonstrates mastery of the standard. 7. **Name It:** • Punch it: succinctly state the key areas the teacher will work on mastering in this planning session. 8. **Do It:** • Perfect the plan. o Plan the overall structure of the unit or week. o Plan the key lessons and student assessments or activities. o Predict the gap: anticipate likely errors in execution and plan for those errors. o ID when observations will take place to see the plans in action and to assess their success.
	Monitor and Follow Up
	Observe for Trends 9. **Observe teaching to ID school-wide and teacher-specific trends:** • Create and use a rubric and set a schedule for review of lesson plan execution—embed as a part of your observation schedule (see Chapter 3, Observation and Feedback). • When observing, evaluate the quality and alignment of the key components of the plan.

LEVER	KEY ACTIONS IN SEQUENCE
	MONITOR AND FOLLOW UP
PLANNING	o Objective aligned to the end-goal/interim assessment
	o Exit Ticket aligned to the end-goal/interim assessment
	o Sequence: lesson fits in a logical sequence of lessons that is building to student mastery
	o Independent practice: adequate time for students to practice the new content and/or skill
	o Modeling or guided discourse: effective instruction aligned to student learning needs
	• ID the pattern of error across a set of lesson plans, homework, or class materials to create a grade/school-wide goal/action step for improving rigor.

Follow Up

10. **Follow up to achieve 90% implementation:**

   • Conduct audits of lesson/unit plans and build plan for improvement.

   • ID individual teachers who have not mastered or are not building effective lesson plans.

   • Plan additional follow-up (modeling, focused planning, extra support).

LEVER	KEY ACTIONS IN SEQUENCE
	PLAN
PROFESSIONAL DEVELOPMENT	1. **Use goals and gaps to plan August PD, yearlong PD calendar, and weekly sessions:**
	• ID highest-leverage topics for PD based on assessment, culture, or observation data and narrow focus to what matters most.
	• Develop yearlong PD calendar that identifies the highest-leverage topics that teachers will need.

LEVER	KEY ACTIONS IN SEQUENCE
	PLAN

PROFESSIONAL DEVELOPMENT

Plan High-Leverage Individual PD Sessions

2. **Create the Do It:**
   - Start from the end: What do participants have to be able to *do* by the end of the session—break it down into the precise steps that they practice (this is your objective!).
   - Script out precise instructions and scenarios to make practice as authentic and effective as possible.
   - Build in sufficient time to "practice perfect": plan, practice, and redo each action that the participant needs to master.
   - Write exemplar script for practice to ID exactly what you are looking for when monitoring.
   - Develop/adapt monitoring tool to track proficiency during practice.

3. **Create the See It:**
   - Design effective activities that allow teachers to "see" an effective model (video, written exemplars, models, etc.).
   - Observe high outliers to ID the strategies and practices that will close the gap.
   - Align each See It activity to the Do It components: they should reveal what teachers have to do.

4. **Create the Name It:**
   - Ask targeted questions before and after the activity that enable teachers to unpack and discover the best practices.
   - Give clear, concise language that describes the core actions teachers need to take.
   - Develop Core Ideas and Name It slides.
   - Design one-pagers of guidance for teachers to help them implement the PD.

5. **Design the follow-up:**
   - Develop clear plans to ensure 90+% implementation of the PD.

Lever	Key Actions in Sequence

| | **PLAN** |

Prepare to Deliver—Internalize the Session Plan

6. **Name your exemplar:**
   - ID what you want participants to say in each section of the agenda: ID when you are looking for the right answer (e.g., leading to a core idea) or the right thinking (e.g., thinking of the right action step for a feedback meeting).

7. **Anticipate the gaps:**
   - ID where participants might struggle, and plan your prompts/facilitation techniques to manage.

| | **EXECUTE** |

8. **Tell a story:**
   - Weave the story between the slides and activities: plan for entry and exit.
   - Say, "We're going to take a journey . . ." or "You hit on many of the key points."
   - Connect each part of the content: "We just looked at ___. The question is how do we do ___? Let's take a look at someone who is doing just that . . ."

9. **Make it clear and concise:**
   - Reduce your words and cut all extra "throwaway" language.
   - Give clear, concise directions, breaking them down to bite-size steps and delivering one at a time. ("Open to page 6 in your handout [wait]. You have 5 minutes to script. Go.")

10. **Punch the core ideas:**
    - Create Core Idea slides to drive home your most important points.
    - Plan your transition into the core idea—"So we've come to a core idea . . ." Say the key line, pause, then say, "Think about the significance of this." Then restate it.
    - Narrate why this core idea is important.

11. **Connect—engage the participants:**
    - Use participant names; use the collective "we."

(left vertical label: PROFESSIONAL DEVELOPMENT)

- Break the plane: circulate around the room.
- Honor their expertise (even when it's not apparent): "Just as Keith said . . ."
- Utilize frequent Turn and Talks to get them to participate in the thinking.
- Ask the "why" during large-group sharing: "Why is this important?" "What is the purpose?"

12. **Bring it:**
- Keep an open face.
  - o Watch your eyes: look at the audience.
  - o Keep your eyebrows up: don't let them furrow!
- Modulate the inflection in your voice to convey excitement.
- Be all in: believe that this is the greatest thing to practice and get right. Don't let your energy drop even if participants aren't excited.
- Use calm, slow hand movements.

13. **Create the illusion of speed with appropriate pacing/time management:**
- Before session, determine which activities can be shortened/ skipped to account for pacing issues.
- Tightly manage transitions, sharing clear instructions for each activity.
- Make strategic on-the-fly adjustments to the agenda based on the pulse or needs of the group.
- Intentionally design reflection time to capture takeaways and help participants write their action steps.

14. **Facilitate discourse when the comments go off track:**
- Roll back: repeat the participant's answer so that she can self-correct.
- Say, "Reactions? What do you think?" Then call on someone who will give a strong answer in response to the off-track answer. Ask that person, "Why is that important?"
- Redirect them back to the core question.

PROFESSIONAL DEVELOPMENT

LEVER	KEY ACTIONS IN SEQUENCE

	EXECUTE

PROFESSIONAL DEVELOPMENT

- o "The key question is how are we increasing student achievement with ___? We have to justify our answer with that in mind."
- o (If the question/comment is about an unrelated subject): "Hold that question. You and I can talk about that at the break. But first I want to answer the question on the PowerPoint slide."
- Wait until the right moment (if the question/comment will be addressed later in the PD): "Great question: we will address that directly in the next part of the PD."

MONITOR AND FOLLOW UP

15. **Actively monitor and follow up to achieve 90+% implementation:**

- Conduct school walkthroughs post-PD and provide real-time feedback on PD objective.
- ID individual teachers who have not mastered/are not implementing the PD objective.
- Plan additional follow-up (modeling, focused observation and feedback, practice, recurring small-group PD).

LEVER	KEY ACTIONS IN SEQUENCE

	PLAN

STAFF CULTURE

1. **Set the vision for staff culture:**

- Name the behaviors you wish to see (connected to belief in the mission and hunger to learn).
- Set clear roles for staff, and weekly schedules.
- Design the meeting/PD where you will roll out your vision.
- Create and use a tracker to track regular positive staff interactions.

LEVER	KEY ACTIONS IN SEQUENCE

STAFF CULTURE	**PLAN**
	2. **Lead PD of your vision:**
	• Develop a concise and compelling story about why you do this work.
	• See It and Name It: give exemplar of the routines and habits that will support positive staff culture.
	• Do It: practice implementing that culture.
	EXECUTE
	3. **Lead by example:**
	• Faithfully implement all the norms of the staff culture.
	• Always state the why: use regular communication to remind everyone of the mission and the important role they play in achieving it.
	4. **Build relationships and be present:**
	• Conduct quarterly/monthly check-ins with staff members you do not regularly coach.
	• Be present and have "small talk" in staff work spaces, at social events, and at other less structured times.
	• ID bellwether staff members and seek their input on staff culture on a regular basis.
	• Respond to harsh feedback/poor staff culture moments with emotional constancy.
	MONITOR
	5. **Assess the quality of staff culture (keep your ear to the rail):**
	• Name key staff members as leaders of that vision and establish regular touchpoints with them focused on staff culture.
	• Administer staff surveys and develop questions based on focus areas identified in data.
	• ID trends in staff survey data and establish 1–2 focus areas to improve.

LEVER	KEY ACTIONS IN SEQUENCE
	MONITOR

STAFF CULTURE	6. **ID and close the gap—create a plan to realign the school to your staff culture vision:** • ID gap between current staff culture and ideal staff culture. • Develop 3–4 high-leverage, specific action steps to respond to poor culture. • Communicate your actions to staff with reference to their feedback. 7. **Lead accountability conversations with staff members who are not implementing the vision:** • State what happened: ask if this assessment is accurate or what they would add/change. • State what was communicated by these actions (e.g., "When you arrived late to PD, you sent a message—even if you didn't intend to do so—that PD doesn't matter or that you don't need it.") • Let the staff member react and state what she was intending/feeling. • State or ID the gap between her intent and what was communicated. • Jointly name the actions to improve for next time.

Pulling the Lever: Action Planning Worksheet

Action Steps for Principals

Self-Assessment

Do a complete assessment of each of your principals. Name their core lever of focus and then the key actions for that lever from the Leverage Leadership Sequence of Action Steps for Principals. Remember:

• For the levers, start with the super-levers (data-driven instruction and student culture), then move to observation and feedback, and then choose any lever that is of highest leverage.

- For the action steps, start with the plan, then go to the next levels (rollout, execute, monitor).

Principal 1: _____
Lever of focus: _____
Key action step(s) for this principal:

_____

_____

_____

Principal 2: _____
Lever of focus: _____
Key action step(s) for this principal:

_____

_____

_____

Principal 3:_____
Lever of focus: _____
Key action step(s) for this principal:

_____

_____

_____

Principal 4:_____
Lever of focus: _____
Key action step(s) for this principal:

_____

_____

_____

Principal 5: _____
Lever of focus: _____
Key action step(s) for this principal:

_____

_____

_____

Principal 6: _____
Lever of focus: _____
Key action step(s) for this principal:

_____

_____

_____

Repeat this activity for each of your principals.

• Is there a pattern across your principals? If so, what would be a great focus for principal PD in order to close the gap on a similar action step?

_____

_____

_____

• What are your next steps for choosing the right action steps for the leaders you coach?

Action	Date

Part 2

How to Coach

Chapter 3

Coaching Data-Driven Instruction

Hand in Hand with the Principal, Part 1

It's 2:30 p.m. at Patterson Elementary School in Washington, DC, and instructional superintendent LaKimbre Brown is making her regular visit to the school. What might surprise you is where you'll encounter her. You won't find her in the principal's office poring over state test data, nor in the hallway observing classes. Today you find her in the conference room, where she has gathered the third-grade team and the principal.

Each of the teachers is wearing the school shirt with the logo "Excellence is the Expectation" on the back. LaKimbre is sitting among them as she kicks off their weekly data meeting.

"Welcome, everyone, to our third-grade data meeting!" LaKimbre greets the team excitedly. "We're going to dive in today into standard 3.OA.1—particularly how to interpret products of whole numbers . . . This is a power standard that we want to focus on. Let's review the protocol for our meeting."

After the group reviews what's about to happen, they begin.

"Read the standard," instructs LaKimbre. "What does a student have to know and do to show mastery of this standard?"

After a minute of reflection, the teachers turn and talk to other and then share out. "They need to understand an array," comments one teacher, "and how they can add on: how that affects the number of groups or the number of objects in each group." Other teachers nod and then contribute additional comments. At the end of a few minutes, they have a list of concepts charted on the wall.

"I see you all came to the meeting prepared with your exemplar," affirms LaKimbre. "Let's look at those together. With your partner, share: What steps did you take to solve this problem? What were the key criteria a student would need to have to show mastery?"

The meeting continues, and teachers dig more deeply into the student work. LaKimbre never once steps away just to observe; she is immersed with them in the student work, and from the warm glances of the teachers, it's clear they know she'll be in it until the end.

 WATCH Clip 2: Brown—See It (Exemplar)—Weekly Data Meeting

LaKimbre Brown hates the word *failing*.[1] Throughout her career in education, she's sought out schools that might typically be labeled that way—places where the vast majority of students are affected by poverty, and achievement levels are extremely low—and transformed them into success stories. In her first school leadership role as principal of Milani Elementary School in Newark, California, she led Milani to incredible gains, with significant growth in student achievement occurring each of the five years she remained at the helm. She then embraced a bigger challenge: she moved to DC Public Schools to lead fourteen schools where 100 percent of the students qualify for a free or reduced lunch. Three years later, ten of the fourteen schools she leads have outperformed the district in growth, and five of those have hit double-digit gains. Figure 3.1 shows a sampling of those results.

LaKimbre's results aren't an isolated case. Further north of her, in Newark, New Jersey, another principal manager achieved outstanding results using the power of data-driven instruction. Juliana Worrell founded Fairmount Elementary School, which went on to be in the top 5 percent of performance in New Jersey. Then she took on the challenge of turning around Alexander Street School, and she transformed it from one of the lowest-performing schools to one of the highest, outperforming even high-income schools (see Figure 3.2).

She, too, took that success to leading a group of elementary schools that are among the highest-achieving schools in their city (see Figure 3.3).

What is remarkable is that these two leaders have never met, but their actions mirror each other and are completely replicable.

Figure 3.1 DC PARCC Assessment, Percentage at or Above Proficiency in Math (top) and ELA (bottom)

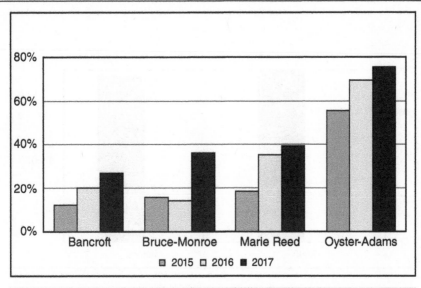

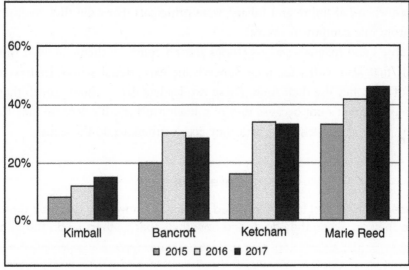

Two things have remained constant in LaKimbre's and Juliana's transition from working as a principal to leading other principals. One is that they still refuse to define any school as failing—and once they've touched a school, no one else can define it that way, either. But the other is that there are still the same number of hours in a day as

Figure 3.2 New Jersey PARCC Assessment: Alexander Street School, Percentage at or Above Proficiency in Third-Fourth Grade

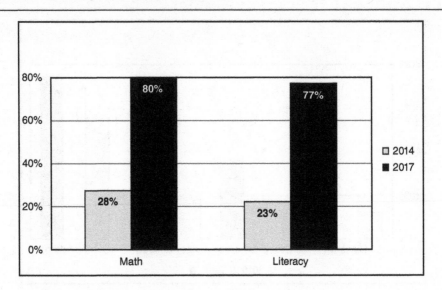

there were when LaKimbre and Juliana were principals. How did they multiply their success from one campus to twelve?

LaKimbre's and Juliana's success stories show a common theme in what works for principals that also works for their supervisors: exceptional school leaders succeed because of how they use their time. These two leaders drive school growth that looks miraculous, but that's not because they're miracle workers. It's because they dedicate their time to what matters most, and they coach others to do the same.

Core Idea

Exceptional school leaders succeed because of how they use their time: what they do, when they do it, and how they coach others to do the same.

If your goal is to get results like theirs, then follow their lead. You will need to strip away as many unfruitful activities as possible and maximize your time on work that has an impact. Let's take a closer look to see how to do that.

We'll start with a deep dive into LaKimbre's and Juliana's foundational practices to build structures and schedules that maximize student learning and make sure principals and teachers do the same.

Figure 3.3 New Jersey PARCC Assessment: North Star Academy Elementary Schools, Percentage at or Above Proficiency in Fourth-Grade Math (top) and ELA (bottom), 2017

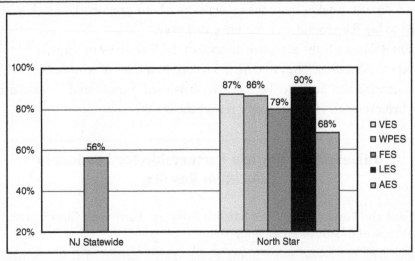

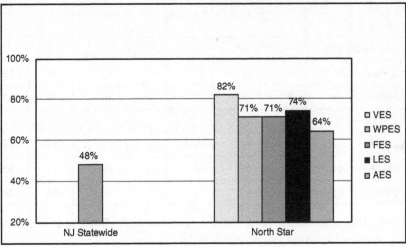

SET THE TABLE: A PRIMER ON THE CONDITIONS FOR SUCCESS DISTRICT WIDE

Talk to any time management expert, and she will tell you that you will not use your time well unless you set it up for success—normally by prepping for your day either at the end of the previous day or in the morning. In other words, you need to lay the groundwork for effective, efficient work.

In many ways, a district or organization of schools functions the same way. But when you lead a district, it takes more than twenty-four-hour prep work to lock in success: you need to lay the groundwork for the entire year.

William Robinson is the executive director of the University of Virginia Partnership for Leaders in Education. The program has helped hundreds of schools from across the country—schools that had once been dubiously labeled "turnaround"—make dramatic gains in achievement. Here are just a few of the results.

University of Virginia Partnership for Leaders in Education Results

Louisiana and Nevada State Test Results: Jefferson Parish and Clark County, Percentage at or Above Proficiency

	Math			Reading			Gains	
School	Year 1	Year 2	Year 3	Year 1	Year 2	Year 3	Math	Reading
Jefferson Parish (LA)								
Gretna Park	36	51	67	47	41	62	**+31**	**+15**
Washington	56	59	72	37	78	74	**+16**	**+37**
Clark County (NV)								
Carson	62	69	76	45	66	76	**+14**	**+21**
Elizondo	44	62	75	38	53	60	**+31**	**+22**
Hancock	58	79	86	49	70	83	**+30**	**+34**

Oklahoma, Utah, Colorado, New Mexico, and Louisiana Results: Proficiency Gains Compared to State Gains, 2013–2016

	Gains	
School	Math	Reading
Westwood Elementary (Caddo Parish, LA)	+24	+31
Fair Park High School (Caddo Parish, LA)	+16	+26
Anadarko High School (Anadarko, OK)	+40	+0

School	Gains	
	Math	Reading
Lincoln Elementary (Ogden, UT)	+27	+20
Manaugh Elementary (Cortez, CO)	+23	+16
Apache Elementary (Farmington, NM)	+37	+34
David Skeet Elementary (Gallup, NM)	+30	+31
Crownpoint Elementary (Gallup, NM)	+25	+30

Early on in the process of working with these schools, William quickly discovered that the first obstacles to school improvement weren't at the school level or principal manager level: they were at the district level. Too many systems that were already in place were inhibiting schools' ability to improve. The starting point for changing the game was to change that situation, building in new systems that would fuel growth instead of limiting it. "If you want to improve school performance, you need to set the table for success," William says.

In Chapter 7 (A Superintendent's Guide to Creating the Conditions for Success), we will talk about overall initiatives that a district can take to drive student success. In this chapter, we will focus on the four action steps that drive data-driven instruction. Depending on your role in your district or organization, you will have more or less control over taking each of these actions. Thus some are actions you can take immediately, and others will require you to work with your district leadership to make these improvements. Before your principals can dig into data-driven instruction at the school level, take on these four action steps at the district level that can set the table.

Action Step 1: Select Quality Interim Assessments

The mission at the heart of all of our collective work as educators is getting students to learn. There is no way to know if students have learned unless you assess it. One of the very first lessons from *Driven by Data* shows us five math problems that are all assessing the same standard but with significantly different levels of rigor. That led to one of the bedrock ideas behind data-driven instruction: standards are meaningless until you define how to assess them. Assessments are the road map to rigorous learning. Thus one of LaKimbre's and Juliana's most important tasks as a principal manager is to make sure schools have access to quality assessments—and are using them to drive curriculum, unit, and lesson planning.

> ## Core Idea
>
> If standards are meaningless until you define how to assess them, then principal management is directionless without district-wide quality interim assessments.

Too many districts stumble at this first core idea, which leads to their not being able to launch categorical change across their schools. The good news is that as of the writing of this book, most districts have some form of assessment tool. The question now has become: How are we to evaluate the quality of those assessments?

A quality set of assessments requires the following characteristics:

Common. All the schools that you lead should have the same interim assessments. Not only are standards meaningless until you define how to assess them, but school data is meaningless if it cannot be adequately compared. Common assessments give you the tools to identify your exemplar teachers and schools as well as find your biggest gaps, which is critical for your leadership (more about how to do that later in this chapter).

Interim. Conducting assessments every six to nine weeks enables you to gauge your schools' performance periodically: not too frequently (which would keep you from really being able to analyze the information) and not too infrequently (which would keep you from seeing if you're making progress). The key to being interim—and valuable—is that the assessments find the right place in your district-wide calendar. They cannot compete with report card night or major celebrations, or teachers will not have time to analyze the results and prepare their reteach. *Driven by Data* provides numerous school calendar examples that you can use as guidance.

Transparent. If assessments are the road map for rigor, then your schools—teachers and leaders alike—need to see the assessments before they start teaching. If they don't see them, they have no way of knowing the level of rigor to which they are teaching! This is one of the biggest obstacles for many districts: they are loath to let go of secrecy because they fear that schools will cheat if they have the tests in hand. What that belief fails to recognize is the purpose of an interim assessment: it's not to evaluate a school but to figure out what to do to improve it! Without transparency, data analysis is impossible—as is quality curriculum planning.

Aligned. Interim assessments are only as valuable as they are aligned to college-ready rigor. Alignment to your state test is an important, necessary step in that direction, but it's insufficient unless the level of rigor the state test sets will prepare students for higher learning.

You can read *Driven by Data* for more details that show how to ensure your assessments prepare students for college, but the following are two fundamentals:

1. Students need to be able to write an argument and essay even if your state test does not require it.

2. Students need to be able to solve problems with the complexity required by the SAT, AP, and International Baccalaureate exams; any high school state test that sets a lower bar than those doesn't prepare the students for college.

Take a moment to assess the quality of your district's assessments (including any gaps).

Stop and Jot

Quality Assessments

Using the criteria discussed in this section, what are the key gaps in your implementation of quality interim assessments?

_____

_____

_____

_____

What are the key actions you need to take as a district to improve the assessments for your schools? What are the changes (if any) that you need to make to your district calendar?

_____

_____

_____

_____

For whatever gaps you have, know that there are a few basic solutions:

- Borrow assessments from another district.

- Build or revise assessments yourselves, either centrally or with teams of teachers.

I have seen districts be highly successful using both of these strategies, and *Driven by Data* gives even more details as to how to engage either approach successfully. Whichever route you take, remember a key lesson from the highest-achieving schools across the country: don't let the perfect be the enemy of good. Get decent assessments in place to enable the analysis-action cycle to flourish, and then you can perfect them over time.

Core Idea

Don't let the perfect be the enemy of the good. A decent assessment can allow you to drive instruction better than no assessment at all.

Action Step 2: Set Up Foundational Curriculum and Lesson Plans

At its most basic level, curriculum is a natural extension of data-driven instruction: teach students what they need, not what they already know. Going deeper, planning is about linking together all of a student's learning to make it rigorous, memorable, and meaningful. What makes that so important? C. Kirabo Jackson and Alexey Malackin from Northwestern University found that giving high-quality plans to weaker teachers had as high an impact as moving their students to the classroom of a teacher in the 80th percentile.[2] In other words, giving newer or more struggling teachers better-quality plans can have as much impact as coaching these teachers to be more effective.

With this in mind, you might discover that one of the gaps in your community of schools is the quality of the curriculum itself—that the curriculum and lesson plans teachers are using shoot well below the rigor of your end-goal assessment. The power of data-driven instruction is that it will expose these gaps. That alone will make major practical inroads, as teachers will start supplementing and improving lesson plans to give students what they need. You may also decide you need to invest in higher-quality curriculum and lesson planning overall.

To identify whether lesson plans or curriculum is the challenge, use these key questions as your guide:

- Is the objective of each lesson aligned to the end-goal assessment that will measure mastery of that objective?
- Does the Exit Ticket match the rigor of the end-goal assessment?
- Does the independent practice give students time to practice what they need?
- Does the modeling or guided discourse set up the students to be successful in their practice?

(If you want a deeper dive into these questions, you can find it in *Leverage Leadership 2.0* in Chapter 2, Planning.)

If your answer is no to these questions, you have two options: support your teachers' and coaches' development as curriculum and lesson planners, or try to acquire a better off-the-shelf curriculum. Beware that the second option has its drawbacks: it is what teachers *do* with the curriculum that will make the difference for your students. Whatever you choose, make sure that the development of teachers' and leaders' ability to revise and implement planning is a core part of your strategy.

Just as was the case with assessments, it's inadvisable to stop all other work on data-driven instruction for the sake of perfecting curriculum. In reality, only by implementing data-driven instruction will you truly find the holes in your curriculum, as you will see what students struggle to learn. But as you advance in your growth as a district, a solid curriculum will be the foundation for long-term success.

Stop and Jot

Curriculum and Lesson Plans

Using the criteria described in this section, what are the key gaps in your lesson plans or curriculum?

_____

_____

_____

_____

What are the key actions you need to take as a district to improve the curriculum or lesson plans for your schools? More training or different curriculum resources?

_____

_____

_____

_____

Action Step 3: Put Schedules and Structures for Data Meetings in Place

With the right assessments and curriculum in place, you can dive into the work of making sure every principal is using those tools to drive instruction. This is where the magic really occurs: when leaders look at student work side by side with teachers to create teaching plans that will improve learning.

However, beware of jumping into coaching data meetings before any structures are in place to ensure that principals can run them on their own. I know of a number of districts in which leaders quickly made weekly data meetings a priority and told their principal managers to supervise them, so principal managers observed their principals leading data meetings when they went to visit the school. Here was the catch: what they failed to realize at the beginning was that these "weekly" data meetings weren't occurring every week, every two weeks, or even once a month. They only occurred when the principal manager came to visit.

Before you can coach around data meetings, you have to make sure they are happening. This is why LaKimbre and Juliana devote time to helping their principals build weekly schedules that lock in regular data meetings for their teachers. Chapter 8 (Finding the Time) in *Leverage Leadership 2.0* dives deeply into how a principal can build effective schedules, providing feasibility tips that clarify how principals can find the time for all of these instructional leadership tasks. You can simply follow those guides to make sure each principal has a schedule that locks in quality data meetings—either in her own schedule or those of her leadership team. The following is an example.

A Principal's Schedule: Prioritizing Culture and Data

Time	Monday	Tuesday	Wednesday	Thursday	Friday
7 AM					
:30	Greeting and Breakfast	Greeting and Breakfast		Greeting and Breakfast	Greeting and Breakfast
8 AM					
:30	Staff Culture Check	Morning Assembly			Morning Assembly
9 AM		1st Grade Weekly Data Meeting	Feedback Meeting		Staff Culture Check
:30			Feedback Meeting		
10 AM	Observe 1st Grade Team	2nd Grade Weekly Data Meeting		4th Grade Weekly Data Meeting	
:30			Observe 4th Grade Team		
11 AM					3rd Grade Weekly Data Meeting
:30					
12 PM		Staff Culture Check			
:30	Lunch	Lunch	Lunch		Lunch
1 PM	Observe 2nd Grade Team				Feedback Meeting
:30		Observe 3rd Grade Team			Leadership Team Meeting
2 PM	Meeting with Principal Supervisor				
:30		Check-in with AP	Feedback Meeting		Feedback Meeting
3 PM			Feedback Meeting		Big-Project Work Time
:30			Feedback Meeting		
4 PM	Dismissal	Dismissal		Dismissal	
:30			PD Session	Staff Culture Check	
5 PM					

As underscored in *Leverage Leadership 2.0*, a strong principal schedule locks in only about 40 percent of that principal's time. The rest is left open for everything else: the students, parents, and events of the day. When principals protect 40 percent of their time for instructional leadership, they have the means to support their school's needs at both the immediate and the long term.

Once each principal has the right schedule in place, LaKimbre and Juliana make sure each of their leaders has the resources to effectively run the data meetings he or she has scheduled. The keys are captured in this one-pager on leading data meetings.

Weekly Data Meeting	
Leading Teacher Teams to Analyze Student Daily Work	
Prepare before the meeting	**Prepare**
	• **Materials ready:** Identify student exemplar; teachers turn in student work, pull and categorize hi/med/lo student work (just a few of each), pull upcoming lesson plan(s) and pertinent prompting guides
	• **Prime the pump:** script the reteach plan and the gap in student understanding; unpack the standard
	• **Preview protocol with teachers:** assign roles, novice teachers speak first, veteran teachers add on and clarify, leader provides additional clarity at end, chart, preview the need for concision from more verbose team members, use of a timer, creation of note-taking template
See It 13–18 min	**See Past Success, See the Exemplar, and See and Analyze the Gap**
	See past success (1 min):
	• "Last week we planned to reteach ___, and we went from ___% proficient to ___%. Nice job!"
	• "What actions did you take to reach this goal?"
	See the exemplar (8 min):
	• Narrow the focus: "Today, I want to dive into [specific standard] and the following assessment item."

See It 13–18 min	**See Past Success, See the Exemplar, and See and Analyze the Gap**

	• Interpret the standard(s):
	  o "Take 1 min: in your own words, what should a student know or be able to do to show mastery?"
	• Unpack the teacher's written exemplar:
	  o "Take 1–2 min to review the exemplar: What were the keys to an ideal answer?"
	  o "How does this [part of the exemplar] align with the standard?"
	• Analyze the student exemplar:
	  o "Take 1 min: How does your student exemplar compare to the teacher exemplar? Is there a gap?"
	  o "Do students have different paths/evidence to demonstrate mastery of the standard?"
	  o "Does the student exemplar offer something that your exemplar does not?"
	
	See the gap (5 min):
	• Move to the sample of unmastered student work (look only at representative sample):
	  o "Take 2 min: What are the gaps between the rest of our student work and the exemplar?"
	  o "Look back at our chart of the standard and exemplar: What are key misconceptions?"

Name It 2 min	**State the Error and Conceptual Misunderstanding**

	Punch it—stamp the error and conceptual understanding:
	• "So our key area to reteach is . . .":
	  o Describe the conceptual understanding
	  o (If needed) Describe the procedural gap (e.g., memorize multiplication tables) and/or missing habits (e.g. annotating text, showing work)
	• Write down and/or chart the highest-leverage action students will take to close the gap

Do It (Rest of the meeting)	**Plan the Reteach, Practice, and Follow Up**

	Plan the reteach (8–10 min):
	
	 • Select the reteach structure:
	
	    o "Should we use modeling or guided discourse?" "Why?"
	
	 • Select the task and ID exemplar response:
	
	    o Select materials: task, text, student work to show-call, what to chart.
	
	    o "What is the ideal answer we want to see that will show we've closed the gap?"
	
	    o (If needed—follow-up question): "What is the 'why' that students should be able to articulate?"
	
	 • Plan the reteach:
	
	    o "Take ___ min and write your script. I will do the same so we can spar."
	
	      ■ **If a model:** write the think-aloud and questions
	
	      ■ **If guided discourse:** select student work for Show-Call, write prompts
	
	    o "Let's compare our reteach plans. What do you notice? What can we pull from each to make the strongest plan?" (Revise the plan)
	
	 • Plan the independent practice:
	
	    o "What will you monitor to see if they are doing this correctly? What laps will you name?"
	
	 Practice the gap (remaining time):
	
	 • "Let's practice."
	
	    o **If a model:** practice modeling the thinking, precision of language, and change in tone/cadence
	
	    o **If guided discourse:** practice Show-Call, prompting students, and stamping the understanding
	
	    o **If monitoring:** practice the laps, annotations, prompts when students are stuck, or stop the show
	
	 • (If a struggle) "I'm going to model the teaching for you first. [Teach.] What do you notice?"

Do It (Rest of the meeting)	**Plan the Reteach, Practice, and Follow Up**
	• Repeat until the practice is successful. CFU: "What made this more effective?"
	• Lock it in: "How did our practice meet or enhance what we planned for the reteach?"
	Follow up (last 2 min):
	• Set the follow-up plan: when to teach, when to reassess, when to revisit this data
	o Observe implementation within 24 hours; teacher sends reassessment data to leader
	• Spiral:
	o ID multiple moments when teacher can continue to assess and track mastery: Do Now questions, homework, modified independent practice
	• Move to the lowest-scoring work:
	o "What students do we need to pull for tutoring? What do we need to remediate?"
	o "How can we adjust our monitoring plan to meet the needs of these students?"

Stop and Jot
Structures for Data Meetings

Do your leaders have the right weekly schedule and resources to hold regular data meetings in their schools? If not, what actions do you need to take to close your gaps?

_____

_____

_____

_____

_____

_____

Note: more details on how to accomplish what's presented in the one-pager appear in Chapter 1 of *Leverage Leadership 2.0*.

How do you make sure that principals use these guides? That's coming up in the next section on coaching; right now just make sure the conditions for success are in place!

Action Step 4: Roll Out PD on Data-Driven Instruction

All of your work around data-driven instruction will feel like swimming upstream if you don't bring the staff along on the ride with you. That's why LaKimbre and Juliana make sure that all of the staff at her schools learn the basics of data-driven instruction: what it is, why we do it, and how (assessment, analysis, and action). You don't have to build this workshop from scratch: you can find everything you need—session plan, PowerPoint presentation, and handouts—in *Driven by Data*. With all these resources at your fingertips, as principal manager, you can take these systems to scale. Any one of your instructional leaders can train all staff—or new hires—in data-driven instruction during teacher orientation. Or each school could lead its own training. Either way, you will enable teachers to understand the journey, which makes the rest of your work so much more impactful.

District-Wide Conditions for Success

Data-Driven Instruction

- **Quality interim assessments**
  - Common across all teachers of the same grade level
  - Interim—at least quarterly and locked into district calendar with time for analysis and action planning
  - Transparent
  - Aligned to end-goal assessments
- **Effective curriculum and lesson plans**
  - Aligned to the rigor of the end-goal assessments
  - Objectives, Exit Tickets, independent practice, and modeling and guided discourse that set up students to be successful
- **Structures for data meetings**
  - Schedules that lock in regular data meetings for the leadership team
  - One-pager on leading data meetings in hands of every instructional leader
- **Rollout of PD on data-driven instruction**
  - Training in data-driven instruction for all staff (or new staff who have not yet been trained)

Note: many of the actions listed in the "District-Wide Conditions for Success" box occur *before* the school year begins, so they can be part of strategic planning for the upcoming school year. By creating these conditions for success prior to the launch of the year, you free yourself to focus on the drivers for learning once the year begins.

Assessments. Curriculum. Data structures. PD. These are the place mats, plates, and silverware that will enable your schools to feast on learning every day. Set the table, and learning will take off.

MONITOR THE LEARNING

For principal supervisors today, the problem is rarely that we don't have data about our schools to look at. If anything, many of us are overwhelmed by having too much: reports on everything from school attendance to pest management compliance. For LaKimbre and Juliana, monitoring learning isn't about whether we have data—it's about whether we have the right data. "It all comes down to: Which standards did they get? Which standards did they not get?" LaKimbre says. If she and the principals she leads can't see that clearly, they're out to sea. "You cannot manage a school for results if you don't know where students are struggling," comments Juliana.

When you manage multiple schools with a myriad of teachers, it often feels very difficult to tune in to what's happening in individual classrooms. You're so many steps removed from them! Yet LaKimbre and Juliana have figured out how to stay on top of learning and gotten it down to a science. And that work is not only transformative but also replicable. Here's how they do it.

A Case Study—See the Right Data

When it comes to reviewing data about student learning, one of the most critical decisions is where to focus. You're responsible for too many schools to dive deeply into every topic for every school in the kind of detail described in *Driven by Data,* so what information will you focus on? Here's a case study that will help us answer that question.

Imagine that you are the principal manager for eight schools. Listed here are your schools' results after the first interim assessment of the year. (Note: this data is built on actual schools' results to make it as authentic a case study as possible.)

You will notice that you have data around the two "super-levers" that make the highest impact on achievement: data-driven instruction (interim assessment scores)

Case Study, Round 1: Reviewing School Results

Review the following data as if these were your schools.
What are your top five actions as a result of this data?

Network Interim Data Dashboard	Target	Network Avg	School A	School B	School C	School D	School E	School F	School G	School H
Interim Assessments	Target	Avg	A	B	C	D	E	F	G	H
ELA IA 5–8	65%	54%	50%	51%	57%	72%	49%	45%	54%	57%
ELA IA Gr 5	65%	59%	52%	50%	60%	73%	53%	54%	71%	59%
ELA IA Gr 6	65%	54%	55%	49%	59%	70%	50%	45%	51%	59%
ELA IA Gr 7	65%	48%	42%	47%	54%	67%	45%	38%	43%	56%
ELA IA Gr 8	65%	55%	52%	56%	56%	78%	49%	44%	50%	55%
Math IA 5–8	65%	57%	57%	57%	61%	72%	50%	46%	57%	61%
Math IA Gr 5	65%	56%	50%	50%	67%	67%	56%	46%	55%	67%
Math IA Gr 6	65%	60%	70%	62%	58%	88%	45%	50%	49%	56%
Math IA Gr 7	65%	53%	53%	54%	57%	63%	51%	42%	49%	54%
Math IA Gr 8	65%	59%	53%	61%	63%	68%	47%	46%	73%	68%
Observation and Feedback										
Number of O/F Meetings (this week)	15		8	8	15	18	7	4	15	12
Number of Feedback Meetings (last 30 days)	50		30	22	45	55	52	15	45	42
Avg Observations/ Teacher (last 30 days)	3		2.00	1.47	3.00	3.67	3.47	1.00	3.00	2.80
% of Teachers with Phase 1–2 Action Steps (from GBF Guide)	15%		50%	45%	15%	15%	80%	75%	75%	10%

School Culture										
School Culture Rubric Score	3		2.2	2.6	2.8	3.8	3.2	1.75	2.4	3.5
Rigor Rubric Score	3		2	2.2	3	3.5	2.8	1.5	2.2	3.3
% of Students Present This Period	95%		94%	94%	96%	95%	97%	92%	94%	95%
% Students Tardy per Day This Period	5%		6%	8%	9%	4%	10%	7%	11%	13%
% of Students Attriting YTD (% of Enrollment)	5%		1%	4%	0%	1.3%	1.8%	2.7%	3.8%	0.8%

and student culture (culture/rigor rubric scores, attendance, attrition), as well as the next most impactful lever observation and feedback (frequency of observations and feedback meetings and percentage of teachers mastering early-phase action steps).

With this data in hand, what are the top five actions you would take to support your schools? Take a moment to write them down before reading on.

Stop and Jot

What are your top five actions as a result of this data?

_____

_____

_____

_____

_____

_____

_____

_____

Answer: I have given this exercise to more than one thousand principal managers across the country, and some common patterns emerge in the responses. When leaders look at this data, they often focus first on the schools that are failing, particularly School F. Their top action steps often include ramping up the observation and feedback cycle and focusing on coaching the large percentage of teachers who are struggling with foundational action steps. And, indeed, actions like these will be constructive when you're working to support a struggling school.

But when LaKimbre or Juliana look at this data, they take a different approach. Here are LaKimbre's top action steps.

Top Action Steps for Case Study, Round 1

1. Observe teachers and leader at School D to determine instructional and cultural systems that are causing higher results.

2. Observe top teachers at other schools—5th grade ELA and 8th grade math at School G, and 6th grade math at School A—to identify best practices.

3. Observe remaining schools with top exemplars (see points 1 and 2) in hand to ID the gaps in implementation.

4. Dive into 7th-grade math/ELA curriculum with content expert(s) to assess weak spots and misalignment.

5. Invite the top-scoring teachers to lead weekly data meetings at a cross-regional PD.

What first jumps out at you is where she starts her work. LaKimbre doesn't go first to the schools that are faltering, but rather to the schools, teachers, and subjects that outshine the rest. She starts with actions that will help her figure out what's going right in her district so that she can replicate it at schools that haven't seen the same successes yet.

LaKimbre teaches us a very important lesson. Too often as principal managers we become firefighters—we run toward whatever is burning most brightly. Lost in this urgency are the questions, What will we do when we get there? How will we solve the problem? Focusing on the bright spots in your schools will point you to the exemplar you are looking for your struggling schools to replicate.

Without an exemplar, you cannot fix the error, because you haven't yet identified what you want it to look like when it's fixed—or what strategies will make it look that way. In effect, you're running to the fire without water to extinguish it.

Now let's take the case study one level further: imagine you've taken this core idea to heart, and you've now made it a point to observe your exemplars first. You've had a chance to implement two of the top action steps LaKimbre listed: you've observed the teachers at School D and then those at the other schools. You've also asked one of your literacy coaches to give you an overall network analysis of the literacy results, as those were weaker overall, and in particular the seventh grade, which had the lowest assessment results of all grades.

During your observations, you have collected a small packet of sample student work from each of your schools—one higher-, medium-, and lower-performing student from each school. On the DVD that accompanies this book, you have access to the complete student work samples. Here we've attached a part of the student work from Schools D (exemplar), F (struggling school), and H (middle achiever). Take some time to read through these student work samples.

Taking into account the original data table for each school and this additional student work and the literacy teacher's analysis, now what are the top five action steps you would take to improve student learning?

Case Study, Round 2: Adding Student Work

The following is student work from seventh-grade ELA.

We've included a few samples from School D and a summary of the student work from Schools F and H.

(Note: you can find the actual samples on the DVD if you want to look more closely.)

School D Sample Student Work (see DVD for full samples).

① PQ: Authors VP + technique

Read the passage. Then answer the questions that follow.

Are Our Nation's Treasures in Danger?

by David George Gordon, Current Science

1   Everybody loves the American outdoors—too much, perhaps, for the outdoors' own good. This year, record numbers of tourists and adventurers are flocking to national parks and wilderness monuments. By their sheer numbers, these people are putting our nation's top outdoor attractions at risk, say experts.

Under Pressure

2   In Wyoming, Yellowstone National Park is being stretched to its limits. So is its Montana neighbor, Grand Teton National Park. Together, the two parks could receive nearly 5 million people—ten times the population of Wyoming—over the course of this year.

3   "The lodging is full, the campgrounds are full. There's nowhere to park," says Scott Moorcroft, a ranger at Grand Teton National Park. "Things get challenging, to say the least," he adds.

4   During busy summer months, park rangers must struggle to serve their guests. At the same time, they must take steps to safeguard the nation's most valuable scenic, historic, and prehistoric treasures. Despite their best efforts, rangers aren't able to protect those treasures all the time.

Illegal Souvenirs

5   Take the case of Petrified Forest National Park. Here, in the midst of northeastern Arizona's famed Painted Desert, are the ancient remains of what was once a semitropical forest, a forest characterized by a warm climate and moist land.

6   Roughly 60 million years ago, the climate became considerably drier. The forest slowly turned into an arid, or dry, desert. As millions of years passed, the soft wood of forest logs was replaced by quartz crystals—a process known as petrification—and the logs turned entirely to stone.

7   Today, though, even with government protection, the attractions of Petrified Forest National Park are not safe. Souvenir hunters are robbing the park on a daily basis. They take with them an estimated 12 tons of petrified wood every year.

8   Signs throughout the park remind visitors that such thievery is against the law, punishable by stiff fines and even prison sentences. When the visitors learn that they may be searched before leaving the park, they often toss their stolen treasure out of car windows. In one month during the park's busy summer season, rangers have gathered as much as 100 pounds of petrified wood that's been discarded this way.

C1: The visitors in national parks cause
Go on trouble for the rangers, are steal and discard stuff then

1. Why did the author likely include the section titled "Hot Attraction"?
   A. To explain what the Old Faithful geyser is, how often it erupts and what the eruptions look like. *Both around into* ~~handwritten~~
   B. To explain how volunteers have been able to help preserve a national landmark. *Detail*
   C. To point out the value of preserving a place like the Old Faithful geyser.
   D. To show how famous and popular the Old Faithful geyser is. *general idea*

2. Which of the following best demonstrates the sequence of claims made in the passage?
   A. The nation's natural treasures are at risk. Too many people attend our national parks. Some people damage national parks out of ignorance. We must protect our national parks for the future.
   B. The nation's natural treasures are at risk. We must protect our national parks for the future. Some people damage national parks out of ignorance. Too many people attend our national parks. *last first*
   C. We must protect our national parks for the future. The nation's natural treasures are at risk. Some people damage national parks out of ignorance. Too many people attend our national parks. *last*
   D. Some people damage national parks out of ignorance. Too many people attend our national parks. We must protect our national parks for the future. The nation's natural treasures are at risk. *first*

3. PART A - How do park visitors influence events in the national parks?
   A. They make the parks too crowded. *which causes*
   B. They do not care about the park's fragile ecosystem. *they do care in Old Faithful*
   C. They produce large amounts of trash like cans and rifle shells.
   D. They damage natural features that need preserving.

4. PART B - Which statement from the text best supports the answer to PART A?
   A. "The lodging is full, the campgrounds are full. There's nowhere to park,' says Scott Moorcroft, a ranger at Grand Teton National Park." [Paragraph 3] *wrong ent*
   B. "For them, it's like walking along a beach and picking up seashells." [Paragraph 9] *missing context*
   C. "They don't realize that their activities are harming the fragile landscapes that attracted them there in the first place,' she maintains." [Paragraph 10]
   D. "People don't realize that about 6.5 meters (6 yards) below the surface, Old Faithful's vent is only 1 meter (3 feet) wide." [Paragraph 16] *context*
   E. "It's part of a park ranger's job to teach people how to act responsibly in the outdoors,' says Chirakawa." [Paragraph 20] *NR*

A. In "Are Our Nation's Treasures in Danger?" and "Underused Parks Work to Create Awareness, Access," the authors present different viewpoints on the role of visitors in national parks. Compare and contrast each author's viewpoint. Use evidence from both texts to support your answer. *B3*

In your answer be sure to:
- Describe each author's viewpoint on the role of visitors in national parks. *B1*
- Explain how each author supports his argument. *B2*
- Use evidence from both texts to support your answer.

Planning Page

You may PLAN your writing for the essay here if you wish, but do NOT write your final answer on this page. Your writing on this Planning Page will NOT count toward your final score. Write your final answer on the following pages.

[handwritten planning notes in table form:]

thesis: David George Garden believes that ignorant visitors are the reason they damage the park that use refers to experts to prove it. Jeremy Rosenthal believes that underused parks should work together ...

4 — David George Garden believes that ignorance of the visitors is the reason why they dominate the park and refers to experts to prove.

B2 — Rosenthal believes that underused parks should work together to create awareness and uses statistics to prove it.

B3 — Both authors believe that visitors and tourist in the park are necessary but they both differ in the reason why

School H Sample Student Work (see DVD for actual samples):

On the School H samples, students underlined a few key sentences on each page and paraphrased those lines in the margin. The multiple-choice questions showed a process of elimination: wrong answers were crossed out. For the essay, there was prework written of key arguments and evidence for each point.

School F Sample Student Work

There were no annotations on any page and no prewriting: just blank pages with only answers circled on the multiple-choice questions.

Case Study, Round 2: Network Analysis

Here is the network analysis of the literacy results that you asked your coach to do.

Network Analysis of Literacy, Particularly Seventh Grade

Central Idea II: *Determine a theme or central idea of a text and analyze its development over the course of the text; provide an objective summary of the text.*

Across the interim assessment, students struggled to identify the best evidence to establish the claim of the text, both in their writing and on the multiple-choice section of the test. Some students missed the central idea and key evidence altogether; others could sometimes choose "just OK" evidence, but frequently did not use that to support their understanding of the central idea.

Some examples:

- **Question 7—Central Idea II (Part B—17%).** Fewer than half of the students who got question 6 correct were able to find the correct evidence to support the answer (53% correct on Q6 dropped to 17% correct on Q7).

- **Question 19—Central Idea II (Part B—20%).** Again, fewer than half of the students who got question 18 correct were able to find the correct evidence to support the answer (47% correct on Q18 dropped to 20% correct on Q19).

- **Writing**
  - **Essay—Evidence (52%).** Students chose evidence that was not completely without merit, but evidence chosen often was not the strongest possible to support the prompt—or was not analyzed in a way that informed the central idea. Although it was less pronounced than at this time last year, students were still struggling with limiting their evidence ("chunk it") to the most critical part.

Other writing gaps:

- At most schools, and across all levels, students did not prewrite for the essay or wrote structures that were extremely loose (e.g., writing the words "Intro, BP1, BP2, Conclusion" or "Restate Thesis" without doing the work of planning). As a result, the following issues were present:
  - Students did not explain the "so what" behind their evidence, just restating the quote or simply explaining it without using it to build on the central idea.
  - Students' evidence selection often provided weak (or improper) support to their arguments, particularly in those cases where it wasn't preplanned.
  - Thesis statements, in some cases, were unclear or vague; they didn't provide a clear, underlying argument for the essay.

Stop and Jot

When you look at the original results of the eight schools combined with the student work samples and network analysis, now what are your top five actions?

Which action steps would you keep the same from the first round, and which ones would you change?

_____

_____

_____

_____

_____

_____

_____

_____

Answer: When I give Round 2 of this exercise to principal managers during PD, many of them make the shift in their action steps to observe exemplar teaching and instructional practices, and some hold on to action steps around observation and feedback and struggling teachers.

The power of looking directly at student work, however, is in the opportunity to go even deeper. Here are four high-impact action steps LaKimbre would take to improve results at these schools.

Top Action Steps for Case Study, Round 2

1. Develop key guidelines for identifying the claim in informational texts:
   - How to annotate to identify key ideas and details
   - How to write subclaims and how to notice shifts in claims
   - How to synthesize a final claim
2. Lead an all-school PD on reading for claim and providing appropriate evidence:
   - Work with School D leader and teachers to develop and lead a cross-campus PD.
3. Create a monitoring checklist for instruction leaders:
   - During walkthroughs with leaders, monitor the percentage of students on task during independent practice:
     - Pen to paper: they are answering questions
     - Annotations: they are annotating texts and tasks with proper evidence and subclaims
     - Answers: they have the right answers
4. Enhance the weekly data meeting with School D exemplars:
   - Add exemplar student responses from School D teachers to all schools' weekly data meetings.

Turn back and compare these action steps with the ones that grew from the previous round of the case study. The first set of action steps seeks to collect data on what happened to student learning; the second set starts addressing the learning itself. By the second round, you have moved from simply observing exemplar teachers and schools to improving students' ability to read for claim. In short, you have moved from evaluating the currently quality of student learning to changing it.

Core Idea

Monitor the learning, not just the process. Get closer to student work, and you move from evaluating student learning to changing it.

The biggest danger facing principal managers is getting so far removed from student learning that you start taking actions that have no direct impact. We will never be able to get to game-changing action without the insights that come from analyzing student work. Follow LaKimbre's and Juliana's lead, and you can move from just monitoring the process to improving the learning—and that makes all the difference.

This is a radical departure from what most principal managers spend their time on. "Looking at student work opens my eyes and gives me an idea of how to coach," comments Juliana. "Looking at student work in a nuanced way is how we succeed," LaKimbre affirms. "That's what enables you to make the adjustments to teaching that will give children what they need." That's precisely why LaKimbre's and Juliana's other actions as a leader are consistently the right ones to drive results in their schools. Monitoring student learning is the cornerstone on which every other step in this chapter is built.

The ripple effect of this core idea is significant. For starters, most of us who are principal managers don't readily have access to data and student work in the way it was just presented in this chapter. Second, we rarely lead meetings with teachers ourselves! So before we can move to these sorts of actions that can improve our schools, we first need to build our own process for having this sort of data in hand. Here's how.

Build the Right Dashboard

In some ways, one of the most challenging parts of your work as a principal manager is cutting through the mountains of data about your schools. "There's only so much information I can focus on," shares LaKimbre. "If I don't narrow my focus, I will drown in data." To prevent this, you need a tool to make school data manageable, what we will call a data dashboard. Here are the keys to an effective data dashboard:

- **Keep it short.** The power of the sample dashboard that we shared in the data case study was that all of the data for eight schools fit on one page. If you need to read ten pages of data before you ever look at student work, you will never get past page 3! Less data is more—when you have the right data. Make it a goal to narrow your dashboard to just one to two pages for every ten schools. This will also force you to be disciplined about what data you will monitor closely.

Network Interim Data Dashboard		Network Avg	School A	School B	School C	School D	School E	School F	School G	School H
Interim Assessments	Target	Avg	A	B	C	D	E	F	G	H
ELA IA 5–8	65%	54%	50%	51%	57%	72%	49%	45%	54%	57%
ELA IA Gr 5	65%	59%	52%	50%	60%	73%	53%	54%	71%	59%

- **Make it measurable.** In *Leverage Leadership 2.0*, we repeatedly mentioned the importance of being able to see the exemplar. To see it, you need to measure it. In the case of a dashboard, when a lever is subjective (like any measure of student or staff culture), you need to create a rubric or checklist or survey that will allow you to measure your success.

School Culture										
School Culture Rubric Score	3		2.2	2.6	2.8	3.8	3.2	1.75	2.4	3.5

- **Focus on the levers.** The fastest way to pare your data down to the most important is to look at the leadership levers. In the opening dashboard, the data was limited to data-driven instruction, student culture, and observation and feedback. These levers tell you so much about a school and are the first places to begin your data analysis. We've shared here the most common metrics that schools use, but you can add your own.

Observation and Feedback										
Number of O/F Meetings (this week)	15		8	8	15	18	7	4	15	12
Number of Feedback Meetings (last 30 days)	50		30	22	45	55	52	15	45	42
Avg. Observations/Teacher (last 30 days)	3		2.00	1.47	3.00	3.67	3.47	1.00	3.00	2.80

Collect Student Work

Once you have your dashboard in place, you can create systems around collecting student work. Something subtle yet powerful about Round 2 of the case study was that we didn't give you a pile of tens or hundreds or thousands of pieces of student work; you only looked at a handful. Here are some keys for ensuring that looking at student work is realistic, even for a principal manager:

- **Go high-medium-low—schools.** If you manage more than five schools, you will not have time to look at student work from all of them. But you can choose student work from your top school (your exemplar), a medium school, and a struggling school. Then you can see how close each of them are to the exemplar and begin to assess the size and nature of the gap.

- **Go high-medium-low—student work.** Just as high-medium-low works for schools, it works for student work samples as well. One of the fastest ways to access student work is to have each school pick just a few student work samples from a given assessment: one or two high-achieving, middle, and lower-performing students. Although the teacher will look at all the student work, you won't have time, and a rough sample will still enable you to see patterns and identify gaps.

- **Put the collection work on your team.** Given your responsibilities as a principal manager or superintendent, you don't have time to collect this student work yourself. But you can absolutely lean on your team to do so. Start by asking principals to collect the work samples from the key grade levels or subjects where the data would be best for a deep dive. Or if you have anyone working for you (e.g., secretary, assistant superintendent, coach), have him or her assemble the work for you.

Stop and Jot

What are the action steps you'll take to build your data dashboard?

_____

_____

_____

_____

_____

What are the action steps you'll take to collect student work?

_____

_____

_____

_____

_____

_____

_____

Analyze Student Work

Another challenging aspect of being a principal manager is that your scope reaches far beyond a single school, and often a single grade span. Where you might have been an eighth-grade teacher and a middle school principal, now you are managing not only middle schools but elementary and high schools as well! How can you look at student work in such wide-ranging subjects and grade spans and actually offer any value? Perhaps even more challenging, if you've only taught math and now you're looking at literacy, where do you begin?

Juliana's solution is quite simple: don't do it alone.

Many networks already have staff members who specialize in particular content areas: a literacy expert, a STEM expert, and so forth. Sometimes that expert is one of your top principals, other times it is a coach or even a top teacher. These experts will be your eyes, and they will help you determine the right course of action. But this will only work if you train them—and break some bad habits.

Too often our educational systems have created a false dichotomy between assessment on the one hand and curriculum and teaching on the other. Because of that, often we have taken our best teachers and instructional leaders and made them coaches of pedagogy rather than learning. In short, they become experts on the cycle of a reader's workshop, but they no longer look closely at student work to make sure students learned.

To be sure, quality pedagogy is important to advance student learning, but if we don't connect it to student work, it won't drive results: we'll build a process and not an outcome. If we want to change learning for students, everyone has to be on the same page. Curriculum, pedagogy, and assessment must go hand in hand.

Core Idea

If we want to change learning for students, everyone has to be on the same page. Curriculum, pedagogy, and assessment must go hand in hand.

To spend your staff's time, as well as your own, on what matters most, leverage these content experts to help you analyze student work. Here are the keys:

- **Start from student work, *not* from pedagogy.** The biggest challenge and risk for many content specialists is the desire to monitor processes and not learning. They start looking, for example, to see if the math class was using effective inquiry-style instruction, but they don't also see whether the students learned. This leads us to entrench ourselves in a given pedagogy rather than do whatever it takes for children to learn. The fastest way to change this problem is to analyze student work *before* looking at how the material was taught. There have been too many "content wars" (e.g., Core Knowledge vs. Constructivism, mathematical fluency vs. conceptual understanding) that aren't rooted in student outcomes. Talk to any great educator—teacher, coach, principal—and she will tell you that as soon as you start from student work, the sharp divisions melt away, and you start borrowing the best practices from all sorts of different approaches.

- **Trust your gut and press for clarity.** When your content specialists present you with their analysis, don't just accept it; look at the student work yourself. If their analysis doesn't make sense to you, trust your gut; sometimes the eyes with less experience can give new insight. At a minimum, you can press for clarity. For example, I am pretty weak when it comes to chemistry. When my Science Department chair presents analysis of the chemistry results, I tell her, "Explain it to me in a way that I can understand. If you don't, it won't be clear enough for your students, either."

- **Create a cheat sheet.** For your purposes, you won't be able to monitor all the standards across all assessments; you can only focus on the highest leverage. Ask your specialists to create a simple cheat sheet that summarizes the gap in student work in the most succinct way possible. The earlier "Network Analysis of Literacy, Particularly Seventh Grade" was an example (see "Case Study, Round 2: Network Analysis" in the previous section).

Think about the power of monitoring the learning. By building a dashboard, collecting student work, and summarizing key student learning actions across your schools, you move away from being a distant manager toward being an on-the-ground leader who is driving results.

With the right data in hand, you can shift your focus to coaching your school leaders to lead data-driven instruction.

COACH BY EXAMPLE: LEAD DATA MEETINGS

Hand in Hand with the Principal, Part 2

It is 2:40 p.m.—ten minutes into the data meeting—and the buzz coming from the third-grade team has not waned.

"The following pieces of student work are from those students who only received one of three points," shares LaKimbre. "What I want you to do is take three minutes: figure out what those students could do, and what was the biggest gap that held them back from the exemplar."

The teachers pair up and pore over three student work samples. A few moments later, LaKimbre pulls them back together. "I'm going to have each pair share out the biggest gap."

The first pair shares their thoughts: "The biggest gap is adding on to the array."

Other third-grade teachers nod, and one of them adds, "We thought the biggest gap was knowing the difference between groups and objects."

"Mmm!" exclaims LaKimbre. "These two gaps are very connected. Let's go back to the exemplar student work. What did the exemplar student do that enabled us to see that he understood this?"

Teachers quickly look back at the exemplar, and one of them comments, "Well, he [the student] labeled the groups and the objects in his array." Others nod.

"Yes!" affirms LaKimbre. "We need to move toward students labeling groups and objects so that they can better visualize the array and how to add on."

"That is the root problem right there," concurs one of the teachers. "That's right!" says another.

"Time to design the reteach," instructs LaKimbre. "What are you going to use: guided discourse or a model, and why?"

The meeting isn't even twenty minutes old, and teachers are already beginning to plan how to teach more effectively. They've moved from talking about the teaching to improving the learning.

When LaKimbre first started coaching her principals, none of them had ever experienced an effective weekly data meeting. The only vision they had for it was from videos that LaKimbre showed them. So when they were tentative about leading the meetings themselves, LaKimbre didn't hesitate: she led the first meetings herself.

What is noteworthy about what LaKimbre did is that she is not alone. As I've studied and observed the actions of the most successful principal managers, I've noticed a similar pattern: they jump in and do the work, whether by leading data meetings at schools on a rotating basis throughout the year or by leading all of them early on until principals have it down. "I was a data meeting machine earlier this year!" LaKimbre laughs. "I was going around training my principals. I led at least three data meetings with each of them." Besides giving principals a clearer model to follow so that they will lead successful data meetings in the long run, leading data meetings yourself comes with an added benefit: you know the reteaching plans yourself! Moreover, teachers don't have to wait until their principal perfects the craft of leading data meetings; they can start changing student results right away. The most successful principal managers don't wait for their principals to figure out data on their own; they do the work with them, side by side.

Core Idea

Don't wait for your principals to figure out data on their own.
Do the work with them, side by side.

This is the single most distinguishing characteristic between principal managers who get many of their schools to succeed and those that don't: they get into the weeds and participate in doing the work. Erin McMahon has been a successful leader across multiple geographies, from her time as a principal in New York City to being instructional superintendent and associate chief of academics in Denver Public Schools. She offers the same insight, saying: "If I only have one hour of my day to spend in a school, I'm going to spend it doing data-driven instructional work with my principal. I will move the needle faster that way than in anything else I do."

If you want your principals to lead effective data meetings, you need to learn to lead effective meetings yourself. Here is a breakdown of how to prepare and how to facilitate, and what makes this form of leadership so powerful for your principals.

Prepare

As the old maxim goes, people follow what you do, not what you say. The same applies to weekly data meetings: the quality of your principals' meetings will be not better than the quality of the model you show them. A few more minutes of preparation can yield hours of effective principal execution.

LaKimbre realized this the hard way. "When I first tried leading weekly data meetings, I thought I could lead them without much preparation. I knew the content and had seen a model, so I thought it would be easy." It wasn't. As LaKimbre filmed herself leading data meetings, she realized an uncomfortable truth that applies to many of us as principal managers: she talked too much. Whenever LaKimbre or any of us doesn't prepare sufficiently, we fill the void with our own voice.

Leading as a principal manager is hard, but principals look to us to be their guide. Here are the best tips for being prepared to model effective weekly data meetings:

- **Use your tools—stick to the script.** The Weekly Data Meeting one-pager presented previously in this chapter (as well as in *Leverage Leadership 2.0* in the chapter on data-driven instruction and on the DVD) has an excellent set of prompts and guidance: use it! Stick to those prompts, and you will save words.

- **Know what you're looking for—plan the reteach lesson in advance.** The essence of great facilitation is to let the participants do all the thinking—but then being ready to step in when they're stuck. The only way to guide a group effectively is to know what you're looking for. This entails determining what you think the most effective reteach plan would be for this set of student work. That will force you to unpack the standard, look at the exemplar, and look at the imperfect student work. That might seem like a lot, and it is. But you cannot simply ask questions; you have to know whether your teachers are on track. Who knows: they might end up developing a better reteach plan than your own—that would be great! But by having one planned, you will be able to offer it when the teachers get stuck.

Why would you devote this much time to prepare for a single data meeting? Because these preparations aren't really for a single data meeting. They are for every data meeting that will take place after you leave the school. They are the model that other teachers and leaders will use to guide their daily practices. Your schools will follow what you do, not what you say. Lead an excellent data meeting at their side, and what you say will be what they do.

Core Idea

Principals will follow what you do, not what you say.
Model a weekly data meeting at their side, and what you say will be what they do.

See It and Name It

With a proper plan in place, the meeting flows naturally. Recall how LaKimbre launches her weekly data meeting in the first video clip of this chapter.

 REWATCH Clip 2: Brown—See It (Exemplar)—Weekly Data Meeting

Stop and Jot

How does LaKimbre prepare her principals to lead a data meeting?

_____

_____

_____

_____

As you can see, once LaKimbre has prepared, she follows the prompts from the Weekly Data Meeting one-pager:

See past success. "Last week we planned to reteach_____and we went from ___ % proficient to ___%. Nice job!" "What actions did you take to reach this goal?"

See the exemplar:

- **Unpack the standard:** "In your own words, what should a student know or be able to do to show mastery?"

- **Unpack the teacher's written exemplar:** "What were the keys to an ideal answer?"

- **Analyze the student exemplar:** "How does your student exemplar compare to the teacher exemplar? Is there a gap?"

Note two other things that LaKimbre does: she makes sure staff chart all their answers, and she always speaks last. Why? Because when we are trying to learn something new, a chart serves as a visual anchor that activates our knowledge and frees our mind to do additional thinking. By having a chart of the unpacked standard and exemplar, the teachers can refer to it when identifying the gap, and their answers become more rooted in conceptual understanding.

The power of going last in each round of sharing is that LaKimbre can add whatever the group is missing. Teachers do all the heavy lifting first; LaKimbre takes them to the finish line if they don't get there on their own.

See the gap. With an unpacked exemplar in hand, your leaders and teachers are now more equipped to get to the heart of the matter: What are the gaps between the exemplar student response and the student responses that don't reflect mastery? We see LaKimbre and her team approach this topic at the end of Clip 2. Now, let's take a close look at how Juliana identifies the gaps in leading her principal Jacobi.

 WATCH Clip 3: Worrell—See It (Gap)—Weekly Data Meeting

Name It

Once you've seen the gap, as Jacobi did at the end of Clip 3, naming it is pretty simple. This is the chance to stamp it to have clarity for planning your reteach. Watch how Juliana names the gap with Na'Jee, another principal whom she manages.

 WATCH Clip 4: Worrell—See It and Name It—Weekly Data Meetings

Do It

Next, Juliana moves to the Do It phase of their meeting. See how that looks in the next video.

 WATCH Clip 5: Worrell—Do It (Plan)—Weekly Data Meetings

Stop and Jot

How does Juliana prepare her principal to lead a data meeting?

_____

_____

_____

_____

As with every lever of leadership, practice makes perfect.

Plan and practice the reteach (8–10 min):

- **Select the reteach structure.** "Should we use modeling or guided discourse?" "Why?"

- **Select the task and identify an exemplar response.** "Let's plan the reteach with the following task. What is the ideal answer we want to see that will show we've closed the gap?"

- **Plan the reteach.** Select materials: task, text, student work to show-call, what to chart. "Take _____ minutes and write your script. I will do the same so we can spar."

- **Plan the independent practice.** "What will you monitor to see if they are doing this correctly? What gaps will you name?"

- **Practice** (remaining time). "Let's practice those new prompts now."

Follow up (last 2 min):

- **Set the follow-up plan:** when to teach, when to reassess, when to revisit this data.

- **Spiral.** Identify multiple moments when teacher can continue to assess and track mastery: Do Now questions, homework, modified independent practice.

- **Move to the lowest-scoring work:** "What students do we need to pull for tutoring? What do we need to remediate?"

Contemplate what just happened. Juliana didn't just prepare the third-grade teachers to reteach the standard: she prepared the principal to lead them. She taught the habits of mind for all of them to repeat this process with every standard. Is that worth the time that Juliana spent preparing and leading? The better question might be: Can you afford not to?

COACH BY DOING: MONITOR STUDENT WORK

Coach by Doing

Monitoring the Learning—Live

Walk into Alexander Street Elementary School, and the buzz of students learning echoes down the halls. Enter a classroom and you'll find Juliana Worrell, principal manager, and her principal Andrew Schaefer observing his highest-achieving second-grade teacher, Na'Jee Carter. Na'Jee is in the midst of his small-group guided reading lesson.

As they are observing, Juliana steps to the side of the classroom to whisper to Andrew. "What did you notice?" she asks. "What were the action steps you see Na'Jee take that we would want to see replicated in the other classrooms?"

Andrew pauses for a moment and looks back at Na'Jee. He replies, "He named what they [the students] were doing well and then he named the fix [the reading skill they needed to improve]. So he named the error to help lead them to correct their own comprehension."

"Great," Juliana confirms. "So we'll go to the first-grade classroom and compare."

They proceed to walk down the hall and watch Andrew's first-grade teacher, where students are not advancing as quickly in their reading comprehension. As they observe, they quickly notice differences between her guided reading lesson and Na'Jee's.

Juliana turns and whispers to Andrew: "So the explicit action step for this teacher would be what?"

"Find the gap [in student work]," replies Andrew. "Aggressively monitor to determine the student error to close the gap."

Juliana nods, and they plan what to do with this teacher to close the gap.

  WATCH Clip 6: Worrell—See It and Do It—Coach by Doing

(Note that in this clip, we see Na'Jee in action as a teacher, whereas the other clips in which he's appeared in this chapter show him in his later role as a school leader!)

Juliana Worrell's track record was already incredibly impressive before she agreed to turn around Alexander Street Elementary School, one of the lowest-performing schools in Newark, New Jersey.

As we mentioned earlier, her success, like LaKimbre's, was no accident: she was ruthless about how she spent her time. And as she move into her new role and handed over the leadership of Alexander Street to her successor, principal Andrew Shaefer, she realized something else: you learn not by listening but by doing.

At the heart of every check-in Juliana has with her principals, she gets them to do the work—and coaches them through it. The result? Alexander Street maintained its success after Juliana departed, because the new principal got better faster. That story repeats itself across all of Juliana's schools.

What guided Juliana was a framework for coaching principals rooted in the same See It, Name It, Do It language of every leadership lever. Let's unpack her meeting with Andrew—and other coaching meetings as well—to see what it looks like.

See It: Start from the Exemplar

Let's recall the core idea from the beginning of the chapter: start from the exemplar, because if you don't, you'll be running to the fire without water to extinguish it. In a powerful way, this is precisely how Juliana starts her meeting with Andrew. They go to observe his best teacher, not his worst. You can rewatch that part of the meeting here.

REWATCH Clip 6: Worrell—See It and Do It—Coach by Doing

Stop and Jot

How does Juliana develop her principal by walking around and monitoring?

_____

_____

_____

_____

Think about the power of this observation. Rather than just observe with one teacher in mind, they are observing with the whole school in mind. Moreover, Juliana is equipping Andrew with a vision for what excellence looks like. Her plan for doing so was simple:

- **See the model.** Observe Andrew's top teacher: "What did you notice? What were the action steps you see Na'Jee take that we would want to see replicated in the other classrooms?"

- **See the gap.** Observe another teacher: "What is the gap between this teacher and your exemplar?" "So the explicit action step for this teacher would be what?"

This tried-and-true formula works in many different situations. Are you working on improving teachers' follow-up after reteaching, particularly how they monitor student work during independent practice? Watch the best teacher in action and then replicate those practices. Do members of the leadership team need to improve the Do It part of their weekly data meetings? Observe the best leader in action and then identify the gaps for the rest. In essence, you've found the fire hydrant, and now you're ready to douse the fire.

Name It—for the Leader and the Teacher

Once Andrew has had the opportunity to identify and name the gap for his teachers, Juliana doesn't stop there. She helps Andrew reflect on the right action step not only for his teacher but also for himself. Watch Juliana lead another of her principals through this same reflection process. In this clip, Juliana asks the principal to reflect on what made her model of what it looks like to lead a weekly data meeting effective.

 WATCH Clip 7: Worrell—Name It—Coach by Doing

- **Name the action step:** "Based on what we discussed today, what do you think the action step for [teacher/student work] should be?"

- **Name the action step for the leader:** "What do you think is your action step as a leader?"

- **Punch it:** "So the teacher's action step is _____" [e.g., identify the student error when monitoring] and your action step is _____ [e.g., give real-time feedback to the teacher to fix the error]."

Do It

All of the work we've been looking at leads to a final critical step: getting the leader better at his own practice. After Andrew has seen the exemplar and identified the gap, Juliana doesn't wait until later to fix it—they do so right away.

Juliana simply steps into the hallway, plans the course of action, and leads Andrew to practice it—live. We see all the trappings of effective teacher and leader development:

- **Perfect the plan before practice.** Use your tools (e.g., in this case, their vision for effective data-driven guided reading lessons) to make a plan.
- **Practice the gap.** Go out and practice coaching a teacher while walking around the school.

In this way, both Andrew and his teacher get better. Student learning is impacted immediately, not a few months down the road.

Core Idea

If a principal implements your feedback during the check-in, student learning is impacted immediately, not a few months down the road.

Follow Up

Finally, it's time for the leader and principal to lock in the progress they've made together. Julie Jackson, the star of the original *Leverage Leadership* and chief schools officer of Uncommon Schools, has been a master of this at every level—teacher, principal, and manager. Watch how Julie locks in the learning with the final few minutes of her meeting with her principal.

 WATCH Clip 8: Jackson—Follow Up—Manager Feedback Meeting

As a principal manager, you are the driving force that ensures principals spend their time on what matters most for learning. The follow-up is how Julie makes sure this principal will be prepared to take the actions that will fuel student achievement after their meeting is complete. Here are the steps she takes:

- **Name the tasks.** Julie takes this opportunity to explicitly list what the principal needs to do next: what materials to complete, what videos or exemplars to create or collect, and so on.

- **Focus on data.** This is also an opportunity for Julie to triple-check that the tasks she and the principal have agreed on are focused on data, closing the loop on what the information they have tells them is highest priority.

- **Set the dates.** As my colleague and time management guru Michael Ambriz would say, "If it doesn't get a date, it doesn't get done." Plan when the tasks you and the principal have agreed on will be complete and when you will monitor them.

Think about the power this type of coaching. Each of these principals has grown from _trying_ to lead data-driven instruction to _achieving_ better results. All it takes is maximizing your time to develop them. These actions are captured in the following guide on how to lead meetings with your principal.

Principal Manager Check-In

A Guide for Developing Principals One-on-One

Prepare	Prepare
	Plan your meeting:
	• (When possible) Do a pre-walkthrough of the school and/or look at the assessment data/student work so that you can plan your agenda.
	• Plan around goal from previous week.
	• Have available leader's current and upcoming plans: observation schedule, meeting scripts, PD plans.
	Have your tools in hand:
	• Universal:
	o Leverage Leadership Sequence of Action Steps for Principals
	o Content-specific one-pagers (e.g., Habits of Discussion, 5–12 Reading, etc.)
	• Data and planning:
	o Data dashboard and interim assessments
	o Weekly Data Meeting one-pager
	o Posted lesson plans with embedded feedback/reteach plans
	• Culture:
	o Student and Staff Culture Rubrics and Student Culture one-pager
	• Observation and feedback:
	o Get Better Faster Scope and Sequence and Coach's Guide
	o Observation Tracker and Giving Effective Feedback one-pager
See It	**See It: Success, Model, and Gap**
	See the success:
	• Look at recent data (student work, culture) and quickly ID progress and next steps.

See It	See It: Success, Model, and Gap
	o "We set a goal of ___, and I noticed how you [met goal] by [concrete actions leader took]." o "What made that successful? What was the impact of [that positive action]?" **See the model:** • Narrow the focus: "Today, I want to dive into [one aspect of one of the leadership levers]." • Name the exemplar. o "What should we see when we [observe the class, look at data, etc.]? What do you want the [class/routine/student work] to look like? What were your goals for [this teacher]?" o "Let's look at [exemplar rubric/upcoming student assessment]. What will teachers/students need to be able to do to demonstrate mastery?" • (If unable to name the exemplar) Show a model—choose one: o Show video of effective leadership/teaching: "What do you notice about [model]? What are the key actions the [teacher/leader] takes that makes her effective?" o Model: "What do you notice about how I _?" "What is the impact and purpose?" o Provide real-time feedback in class: "When I intervened, what did I do? What was the impact?" o Read a one-pager or prompting guide: "What are the essential elements of _____?" **See the gap:** • Ask "What is the gap between [end goal/model] and what we saw today?" • Ask "What is causing the gap? What is the challenge in implementing this effectively?" • (If unable to name the gap) Present the evidence. o Present time-stamped video of leader: "What is the teacher/student doing? What are you doing?" "What is the gap between what we see in this video and the [exemplar]?"

See It	See It: Success, Model, and Gap
	o Present evidence: "The teacher is not writing anything down during your meeting. How does this impact the likelihood of her implementing your feedback?"
Name It	**Name It: High-Leverage, Measurable, Bite-Size Action Step**

Name the action step:

- (When applicable) For the *teacher/student*: "Based on what we discussed today, what do you think the action step for [teacher/student work] should be?"
- For the *leader*: "What do you think is your action step as a leader?"

Punch it:

- "Let's stamp it with precise language."
- (When applicable) "So the teacher's action step is __ [e.g., What to Do directions]."
- "And your action step is __."
  - o *What* the leader will work on (e.g., plan before you practice during feedback meetings)
  - o *How* the leader will execute (e.g., "1. Give them two minutes to prepare a script. 2. Review and revise the script. 3. Add additional scripting for anticipated challenges.")
- "In your own words, tell me your action step . . . Let's write that down."

Do It	**Do It: Plan, Practice, Follow Up**

Plan before practice:

- Script the changes into upcoming plans (for meetings or observations).
  - o "Where would be a good place and time to implement this next week?"
  - o "What are all the actions you need to take/want to see in the teachers?"
  - o "Take three minutes to write up your plan."
- Push to make the plan more precise and more detailed.

Do It	Do It: Plan, Practice, Follow Up
	o "What prompts will you use with teachers that we can practice today?" o "Now that you've made your initial plan, what will do you if [key challenge: e.g., resistant teacher]?" • (If struggling to make a strong plan) Model for the leader and debrief. o "Watch what I do and say as I model __." "What do you notice about how I did __?" • Perfect the plan. o "Those three steps look great. Let's add __ to your [script/meeting plan]." **Practice:** • Round 1: "Let's practice" or "Let's take it live." o (When applicable) Stand up/move around to simulate the whole-school leadership feeling. o Pause the role play at the point of error to give immediate feedback. o Repeat until the practice is successful. • Additional rounds: master it while adding complexity. o "Let's try that again, but this time I will be [teacher X who is slightly more challenging]." • (Once mastered) Lock it in. o "Let's look back at our action step. Did we master each part of it?" o "Let's reflect on this role play. What made you successful? Why is that important?" **Follow up:** • Name the tasks: both leader and supervisor write down all tasks with deadlines. o Completed materials: when leader will complete revised plans/materials o Manager observation: when you'll observe the leader

Do It	Do It: Plan, Practice, Follow Up
	o (When valuable) Leader observation of master teacher/leader: when she'll observe master teacher/leader live or via video implementing the action step
	o (When valuable) Self-video: when you'll video leader to debrief in future meeting
	• Set the dates.
	o "When would be the best time to observe your implementation of this?" *or* "When I review your plans, I'll look for this modification."
	o Newer leader: "I'll come in [later this week] and look for [evidence of change]."
Plan Time	**Plan the Use of Time**
	Plan leader's schedule for upcoming weeks:
	• "Based on your successes and challenges this week, how would you adjust your weekly plan?"
	• "Based on today's check-in and your new action step, let's adjust your weekly plan."
	• "Where will this be difficult to follow? How can you set yourself up for success?"

CONCLUSION

Throughout this chapter, we saw the power of finding an exemplar and following it. LaKimbre, Juliana, and Julie are all exemplar leaders we can look to and discover how to drive learning.

At the end of the day, the fruit of this work is seen most clearly not in the overarching results but in the growth of a single teacher: Camille Townsend.[3] Using the systems in this chapter, LaKimbre recognized Camille as an exemplar instructor and urged her to coach her fellow teachers as well. "Her classroom was like heaven, right in the middle of a really tough school," LaKimbre recalls. "Her students were joyous, she had results you could see—she had it all." Now, Camille is a principal herself, sharing her strengths with her colleagues by analyzing data with them regularly. LaKimbre is blown away by the results. "When I go and listen to the way in which her teachers now talk about data, it's in a way that simply was not happening a year ago," LaKimbre says.

By staying close to student learning and the teachers who were fueling it, LaKimbre instigated a seismic shift in the way her principals looked at data. What's more, she gave principals like Camille the tools to become leaders in their own right. As a leader of school leaders, you cannot be present in every school at every moment—but the beauty of this is that you can pass the torch of leadership to other educators. Monitor what matters most, coach on what matters most, and you'll build schools where every student learns the most.

Leverage Leadership Sequence of Action Steps for Principals

Data-Driven Instruction

LEVER	KEY ACTIONS IN SEQUENCE
	PLAN
DATA-DRIVEN INSTRUCTION	**Assessments and Curriculum—Align the Rigor** 1. **Lock in quality interim assessments:** • ID the end-goal assessment (state test, college entrance exam, college assessment) that exemplifies what successful students should know and be able to do. • ID essential content and rigor that students must master for success on end-goal assessment. • Acquire or develop effective interim assessments (IAs) that are aligned to end-goal assessments. • Develop a common IA calendar that identifies when IAs will take place, who and what will be assessed, and when IA data analysis meetings will take place. 2. **Lock in high-quality lesson plans and curriculum materials that align to the assessments:** • See Planning section for details. **Data Meetings—Tools and Structures for Weekly Data/IA Meetings** 3. **Establish essential data meeting structures that result in evidence-based action planning:**

Lever	Key Actions in Sequence
Data-Driven Instruction	**Plan**
	• Create meeting schedule to conduct data meetings to analyze IA data (every 6 weeks) and to conduct weekly data meetings (WDMs). • Establish consistent protocols and prework expectations for effective analysis meetings (e.g., IA analysis meeting protocol, WDM analysis protocol). • Develop a system to regularly collect high, medium, and low samples of student work (e.g., Exit Tickets, spiral review) to use as evidence to ID trends in student learning. 4. **Create effective principal monitoring tools for all post-assessment action plans, including:** • Develop an action plan tracker that identifies teacher reteach goals, timeline, and focus area. • Create systems to have access to assessments and/or DDI action plan when observing. • Create observation schedules to observe teachers in reteaching implementation.
	Roll Out
	PD on Data-Driven Instruction (DDI) 5. **Roll out PD for data-driven instruction:** • Plan and roll out PD on DDI, the power of the question, and writing exemplars. • Develop and roll out exemplar IA analysis to set clear expectations for teacher analysis. • Create repeated opportunities during PD to practice analyzing student data/work and creating 6-week action plans (IAs) or targeted reteach plans (WDM).
	Execute
	Analyze for Trends 6. **Conduct a deep analysis of the data to ID school-wide and teacher-specific trends:** • Find the overall trend.

LEVER	KEY ACTIONS IN SEQUENCE
	EXECUTE

<table>
<tr><td rowspan="20" style="writing-mode: vertical-lr">DATA-DRIVEN INSTRUCTION</td><td>

- o For IAs: ID school-wide patterns in the data: outlier teachers and students (low and high) and key standards that need focus.

- o For WDMs: review the student work to select the highest-leverage standards or question to focus on for analysis.

- ID the key conceptual understanding and error for a given standard or task.

  - o Determine what students should be able to do and say to demonstrate mastery of the standard or task.

  - o ID the key gap between the ideal response and student work: both the key procedural errors and conceptual misunderstandings.

  - o Determine the highest-leverage action steps to take to close the gap.

Data Meetings—Lead Effective Weekly Data and IA Analysis Meetings with Teachers

7. **Prepare:**

   - Narrow your focus: pick the assessment item and student work in advance that highlight key errors.

   - Prepare the exemplar and write your meeting script to ensure an effective, efficient meeting.

8. **See It:**

   - Start with the standard(s): unpack the key parts of the standard that align to the student error to ID the most essential conceptual understandings that students must master.

   - Unpack the teacher and student exemplars (or rubrics) to ID how the work demonstrates mastery of the standard.

9. **Name It:**

   - Punch it: succinctly restate the key procedural errors and conceptual misunderstandings, then have the teacher repeat them and write them down.

10. **Do It:**

    - Perfect the plan before you practice.

</td></tr>
</table>

Lever	Key Actions in Sequence
	Execute

- o Plan the structure of the reteach: modeling or guided discourse.
- o ID the steps, student materials, and students to monitor.
- o Predict the gap: anticipate likely errors in execution and practice that part of the meeting.
- Practice the gap.
  - o ID the most essential elements of the reteach for the teacher to practice, especially the parts that will be hardest to master.
  - o Prompt the teacher to "go live" and practice the prompts that will be used during the reteach.
- Build an effective follow-up plan.
  - o ID when to teach, when to reassess, and when to revisit this data.
  - o Embed the action plan into upcoming lessons and unit plans.
  - o ID when observations will take place to see plan in action and how it will be assessed.

Monitor and Follow Up

11. **Actively monitor implementation of action plans:**
- Observe the reteach.
  - o Start from the exemplar teacher and observe same-subject teachers back-to-back.
  - o ID the gap between the exemplar teacher and other teachers.
  - o ID the gap between the original plan and execution and between student work and exemplar.
- Observe weekly data meetings (WDMs) of other instructional leaders (live or via video).
  - o ID the patterns across meetings and the key areas of growth for the leader's facilitation.
- Track implementation of 6-week action plans and student outcomes following reteach.

(Left vertical label: Data-Driven Instruction)

LEVER	KEY ACTIONS IN SEQUENCE
	MONITOR AND FOLLOW UP
DATA-DRIVEN INSTRUCTION	o Have teacher post lesson plans and/or 6-week action plans in the classroom to be able to observe both the plan and the execution to ID gaps. • Create system for teacher teams to collect student work between WDMs. 12. **Monitor student work in each class using a sequence:** • (A) pen-to-paper, (B) annotations/strategies, and (C) right answers

Pulling the Lever: Action Planning Worksheet

Coaching Principals on Data-Driven Instruction

Network/District Assessment

• Review the district conditions for successful implementation of data-driven instruction (as discussed in the first section of the chapter): Which are the key actions you need to take as a network of schools?

_____

_____

_____

_____

Self-Assessment

• Review the Leverage Leadership Sequence of Action Steps for Principals (embedded throughout the chapter; the full list can be found at the end of Chapter 2, and a print-friendly version is in the DVD appendix).

• Which action steps do you want to target this year as you develop your principals?

_____

_____

_____

_____

Planning for Action

- What tools from this book will you use to lead your schools? Check all that you will use. (All are available on the DVD unless noted otherwise.)

  ☐ Network dashboard sample

  ☐ School dashboard sample

  ☐ Managing Principals to Results one-pager

  ☐ Weekly Data Meeting one-pager

  ☐ Principal Manager Check-In one-pager

  ☐ PD on data-driven instruction for principal managers

  ☐ PD on data-driven instruction for principals (see *Driven by Data*)

  ☐ Other: _____

- How will you modify these resources to meet your district's needs?

  _____

  _____

  _____

  _____

- What are your next steps for coaching principals on data-driven instruction?

Action	Date

Chapter 4

Coaching Student Culture

It's 7:27 a.m. at Ewing Marion Kauffman School in Kansas City, and the halls are still mostly quiet before the upcoming arrival of students. All the sound is coming from a single classroom, where teachers have gathered for a daily ritual called the morning huddle.

Teachers are clustered around the room, engaging in animated small talk. As the clock strikes 7:30, one of the members of the leadership team raises her hand, and the teachers quickly settle into their seats.

"First we have a shout-out to start our day. Welcome back, no longer Ms. Deed but now Mrs . . . Smith!" Teachers warmly applaud and call out words of encouragement to welcome their peer back from her wedding weekend. A few more affirmations are called out before the leader shifts their attention to the paper on each of their desks.

"In front of you is your daily memo. Take one minute to read the announcements." No more words are spoken—nor are any needed. Silence ensues as the teachers review the reminders about field trips, uniforms, schedule coverages, and other small changes to the day.

A minute later, the leader reengages the group. "As you know, we are going to shift our focus to aggressive monitoring during independent practice. Sheila and Lauren are about to model for you how to launch independent practice and monitor students. Watch what words they use, their body language, and what data they collect on their clipboard."

Without a second more delay, Sheila and Lauren stand at opposite corners of the room, each modeling for half of the fifty staff members. The teachers focus intently on one of the two models.

"Time!" calls the leader. "Thank you Sheila and Lauren for modeling! What did you see them do and say?" Teachers call out answers and snaps can be heard around the room. "Now it's your turn to practice. You have all the steps Sheila and Lauren took right on the paper in front of you, as well as what room you will be in for practice. Good luck!"

Without another word, all the teachers immediately head out the door and form in groups of three or four in each of the classrooms on that hallway. As soon as they are gathered, one of the teachers begins to follow the model. "Nice work, Emily!" affirms the instructional leader who is observing that classroom. "Don't forget: keep your body facing the majority of the students. When you come back to the front of the room, walk backwards so you can keep your eyes on them."

Thirteen minutes later, morning huddle has ended. But not before every teacher in the school has practiced the launch for independent practice three to four times each. And not before every classroom at Ewing Marion Kauffman just got a little bit better.

 WATCH Clip 9: Lofthus—Do It—Practice Clinic
Note: Not on DVD—see Contents for unique link to this video.

When you step into one of Hannah Lofthus's schools, you sense right away that she's gotten culture right. There's a focused energy that reverberates throughout the Ewing Marion Kauffman Schools, with students and teachers alike going about their daily tasks both purposefully and joyfully. There's a shared understanding that learning is urgent in these schools, and that understanding is palpable.

The results show. In 2015, Kauffman was named the best public school in Missouri.[1] Most of Kauffman's students entered fifth grade (their starting grade) achieving an average of three years below grade level. Today, they've not only closed the achievement gap but eradicated it. In Figure 4.1, you can see how the Class of 2023 grew over a five-year span.

Among Kauffman eighth graders, 81 percent scored proficient in math on the state assessment—triple the statewide average.[2] Visit the school today, and these impressive results have persisted.

Hannah is quick to acknowledge the role culture plays in getting results like these. "Ninety percent of the time, the teachers with the best culture are having the highest

Figure 4.1 Missouri State Assessment: Kaufman School Class of 2023, Percentage at or Above Proficiency

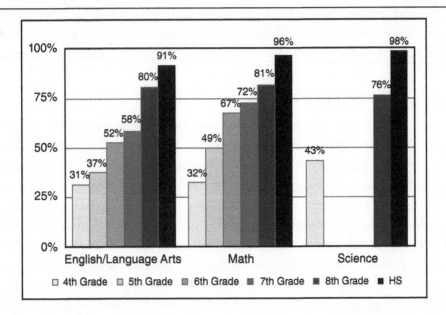

achievement," she states. Hannah and the leaders she coaches are succeeding because she lives by the credo that culture is what you see in your schools, not what you hope for—and that what you'll see in your schools will be what you have practiced.

Core Idea

Student culture is what you see, not what you hope for.
To see what you hope for, you have to practice.

Spotting an incredible student culture is the easy part. What's far more difficult is to build one—to know what schools like Kauffman do to get there. How does Hannah do this? By giving principals and teachers alike abundant opportunities to practice.

The morning huddle is just one example of this. In the vignette that opened the chapter, the principal didn't even have to lead it: the culture was so established that other members of the instructional leadership team could direct the teachers. They keep announcements quick and focus the bulk of their time on doing what it takes to get better. "Every week, we pick action steps to master by Friday," Hannah says. "Practicing them during the morning huddle gives everyone an extra opportunity for development every day."

In this chapter, we'll lay out the ways Hannah coaches her principals at the Kauffman Schools to practice the student culture they all dreamed of. Practice is what makes those dreams become reality.

TRAIN THE ROLLOUT

In traveling the country talking to principal managers, I heard a common refrain over and over: 90 percent of the culture of a school can be traced back to what happened in Week 1. When a school doesn't start well, it becomes incredibly difficult to fix later in the year. Jarvis Sanford of the Academy for Urban School Leadership, a turnaround organization in Chicago, confirms this: "I can predict a schools' turnaround success just by watching the first day of school. If a leader doesn't set the expectations right from the beginning—and hold students and staff accountable to them—they won't be able to do so later." Hannah agrees: "If we meet our goals for student culture, we win the year."

This is why top principal managers like Hannah don't wait until culture is struggling before they act. The majority of the work it takes to build culture at Kauffman happens *before* the first day of school. Remember: you never get a second chance to make a first impression. If you roll out culture effectively, you'll carry it all the way through the year.

> ### Core Idea
>
> You never get a second chance to make a first impression.
> Prepare your rollout, and you'll carry your culture.

Some principals get student culture working very quickly and can conduct an effective rollout with minimal additional guidance; others will need more support. That is where you come in. So how do you coach your principals to roll out student culture effectively? It starts with knowing what you're looking for.

Start from the Exemplar

Let's recall from *Leverage Leadership 2.0* what an effective rollout should look like. In the clip here, school leader Tera Carr from Hamilton Elementary School in Tulsa is leading a rollout of entry routines.

WATCH Clip 10: Carr—Do It—Roll Out to Staff (Principal Clip)

Stop and Jot

How does Tera roll out student culture to her staff?

_____

_____

_____

_____

Tera took the following key actions (you can find more detail on these actions in *Leverage Leadership 2.0*):

Model (See It):

- **Hook.** Let your staff know why this matters: short and sweet.
- **Frame.** Name what will happen in the model and what to look for.
- **Model.** Exaggerate the model of the routine: body language, tone, and precise language.
- **Debrief.** Stamp the understanding of the model by asking the staff to unpack what they saw.

Practice (Do It):

- **Give precise directions.** Make it clear where and how to practice.
- **Practice perfect.** Give teachers the chance to practice, get feedback, and try again.

Tera succeeds by making sure she models what she needs her leaders to do—and getting them to practice it themselves.

So how do you coach a principal to have as effective a rollout as Tera? It looks strikingly similar to Tera's clip, only this time you are practicing *leading* the rollout! Let's take a look at Hannah doing just that.

 WATCH Clip 11: Lofthus—See It and Name It

Hannah follows the same steps for managing principals around student culture that we saw Juliana Worrell use in coaching instruction:

- **See the success.** Hannah starts by naming where the principal had succeeded in implementing previous feedback.
- **See the model.** Hannah stands up and models what an effective rollout should look like. In doing so, she enables the principal to see precisely what to do.
- **See the gap.** She asks, "What is the gap between what I modeled and what happened today?"
- **Name the action step.** "Based on what we discussed today, what do you think the action step for [teacher/instructional leader] should be?" "What do you think is your action step as a leader?"

Core Idea

When coaching principals around culture, follow the same formula:
See the model. See the gap. Name It. Do It.

Do It

Once they've seen the model and the gap, principals get so much better when they practice! That's why if you walk into the Kauffman Schools prior to the start of teacher orientation, you will find principals practicing their rollouts—with Hannah, with each other, and on their own. They practice every part so that they leave nothing to chance. Remember: every minute spent perfecting the rollout yields thousands of minutes of quality culture for the rest of the year!

MONITOR CULTURE

Once you've rolled out your vision for culture to your staff, you'll need to walk through your campuses to monitor how well that vision has been implemented. Because culture is what you see, this is the easiest part. You can walk into the school immediately and see if the culture is on track. What's difficult is deciding what to do about it if it isn't.

To set herself up for success in that more challenging task, Hannah conducts her student culture walkthroughs with a culture rubric in hand—a strategy that began, as so many great strategies do, with a challenge. "One leader's student culture wasn't meeting our bar," Hannah recalls. "I wondered, why isn't this working? I'm telling her to do everything I'm doing. To figure out where the breakdown was and how to support her, I built a student culture rubric and started going room-to-room with it." The rubric gives Hannah the ability to immediately codify the evidence she sees defining her schools' culture, which means that later, she'll be prepared to codify each school's next steps.

Whether you're perfecting instruction or culture, what you assess determines what you'll work on. "We spend a really inordinate amount of time determining how we'll measure things," says Hannah, "because we really believe, if you can't measure it, you can't do it."

Core Idea

If you can't measure it, you can't do it.
What you assess determines what you work on.

Here's a sample of what rows on a rubric could look like (you can find a full rubric on the DVD):

Monitoring Culture

Student Engagement and Strong Voice

School-Wide Systems	Advanced	Proficient	Working Toward	Needs Improvement
Student Joy and Engagement	• Students seem to be joyful and excited to be in school. • 90–100% of students are engaged in classroom activities. • Older students internalize and model behavioral expectations without teacher supervision. • 100% of students exhibit professional posture.	• Most students seem to be joyful and excited to be in school. • 80–90% of students are engaged in classroom activities. • Older students internalize and model behavioral expectations with minimal teacher supervision. • 90% of students exhibit professional posture.	• Although many students seem joyful, there are notable instances of student arguments and/or lack of joy. • 70–80% of students are engaged in classroom activities. • The older students have not internalized behavioral expectations and are resistant to those expectations. • 70% of students exhibit professional posture.	• Students generally seem disinterested in school. • Less than 70% of students are engaged in classroom activities. • The older students have not internalized behavioral expectations and are more resistant to those expectations than younger students. • Less than 70% of students exhibit professional posture.

School-Wide Systems	Advanced	Proficient	Working Toward	Needs Improvement
Strong Voice	• Economy of language: minimal language is used to build student compliance. • Don't talk over students: adults never talk over student chitchat. • Do not engage: adults never engage student excuses/distractions during correction of student misbehavior. • Nonverbal authority: adults always use square up/stand still and proximity to maintain student compliance. • Quiet power: teacher always speaks slowly and quietly.	• Economy of language: minimal language is used to build student compliance. • Teachers/leaders rarely allow student side conversations while talking. • Teachers/leaders rarely engage student excuses/distractions during correction of student misbehavior. • Nonverbal authority: adults almost always use square up/stand still and proximity to maintain student compliance. • Quiet power: teacher almost always speaks slowly and quietly.	• More language is used than needed to build student compliance. • Teachers/leaders sometimes allow student side conversations while talking. • Teachers/leaders sometimes engage student excuses/distractions during correction of student misbehavior. • Nonverbal authority: adults sometimes use square up/stand still and proximity to maintain student compliance. • Quiet power: teacher sometimes speaks slowly and quietly.	• Teachers are so verbose that students do not understand compliance requested. • Student side conversations often occur while teacher is talking. • Teachers/leaders often engage student excuses/distractions during correction of student misbehavior. • Nonverbal authority: adults rarely use square up/stand still and proximity to maintain student compliance. • Quiet power: teacher rarely speaks slowly and quietly.

You'll notice that any effective culture rubric is set up to monitor both student and adult actions. As successful leaders across the nation have wisely noted, it's the adults, not the students, who ultimately create the culture of a school. "A struggling culture is an adult problem," notes principal manager Rebecca Utton of Denver, Colorado. "The good news is we're the adults, so we can fix it."

Following the same philosophy, Hannah monitors what students are doing to find where a culture breakdown is happening. But she monitors adults to find out *why* it's happening—and how to fix it.

Core Idea

Monitor students to see where the breakdown is happening.
Monitor teachers and leaders to see why.

Stop and Jot

What is the quality of the tools and/or rubrics that you currently use to measure student culture? What improvements could you make?

_____

_____

_____

_____

You've now trained the rollout and monitored the culture. How do you close the gaps once the year has launched? Hannah does that in two ways: coaching while walking around, and coaching during a meeting. Let's take a closer look at both.

COACH BY WALKING

When you're coaching a leader around student culture, opportunities to coach are . . . everywhere. All a principal has to do is step out of the office (and sometimes student culture will even find you there!), and student culture awaits. From observing disengaged students in a classroom to a hallway routine to breakfast, lunch, or dismissal, a principal has countless chances to lead.

This is what makes coaching by walking around a school with the principal so powerful. You get to assess the quality of the principal's leadership in real time, and the leader can implement your feedback right away with the students and teachers in action.

Jesse Corburn, assistant superintendent for high schools at Uncommon Schools, has seen the power of coaching this way: "Your action step sticks when your principal has a chance to implement it right away. You create muscle memory." Here is Jesse working with his principal Ashley Anderson to use real-time feedback to improve student culture in the classroom. They are particularly focused on working with her teachers on the action step of "teacher radar" in the Get Better Faster sequence of action steps: how to scan the room for off-task behavior. Watch how Jesse coaches Ashley to improve her real-time feedback:

WATCH Clips 12 and 13: Corburn—Do It (Coach by Walking)

The process Jesse and Ashley follow in a teacher's classroom is strikingly similar to the one they would follow if they were in an office: See It. Name It. Do It. Here's a summary of how they vary this process to make it work well during a walkthrough.

- **See the model.** Jesse gets Ashley off on the right foot by making sure she is clear on what this skill will look like when she practices it correctly. You can do this either by agreeing with the teacher on it in advance or by modeling it for her in real time, following the guidelines for real-time feedback outlined in *Get Better Faster* and *Leverage Leadership 2.0*.

- **Do It 1—identify the gap.** The first time Ashley tries practicing the skill—again, using the guidelines for constructive real-time feedback—serves two purposes. First, it gives her a chance to practice the skill right away. But it also gives Jesse the opportunity to identify the gap in implementation that Ashley is struggling with. That way, he can debrief with her about that particular challenge before having her practice again.

- **Do It 2—practice the gap.** Ashley's second round of practice is more targeted, with Jesse having her specifically zero in on the gap they identified in the first Do It. Giving Ashley additional opportunities to perfect what she's struggling with is how Jesse ensures she'll be prepared to do what's most difficult for her when she walks through the school without him. Any additional rounds of Do It are opportunities for Ashley to perfect the gap she practiced. Getting the skill just right, and practicing it just right more than once, are what will make this skill into a habit Ashley can use to maintain student culture with consistency.

What makes this exchange particularly impactful is the way Ashley is able to overcome her initial discomfort. Often when a leader is working on developing a new skill, she can appear resistant to the feedback. Principal managers can easily start to believe that leaders don't want to improve or, even more extreme, that they don't believe in the mission or in the children. What these managers forget, however, is that most resistance is rooted in failure: a lack of experience of being successful that leaves a person resigned to feeling that it is not possible.

In the moment that Ashley finally experiences success, it changes her belief about what she can do. Rather than trying to confront Ashley's beliefs on a philosophical level, Jesse just focuses on building her skill. He doesn't need to wait for Ashley's "will" to build the skill. Rather, building the skill creates the will.

Core Idea

Build the skill to build the will.

When you take advantage of every moment walking around the school to coach your principal, you build her skill. Little by little, you change the leader—and the school—for the better.

COACH BY MEETING

Sometimes a leadership skill in student culture is a bit too complex to master while walking around. In those cases, you can go to the principal's office and coach him in a quieter, more controlled setting. The process of coaching, however, follows a similar format.

See It and Name It

Take a look at this video of Hannah meeting with one of her principals. They're discussing a specific conflict that recently occurred with a student at this principal's school. The student in question stole a bottle of lotion from another student, and refused to return it even after acknowledging what she did.

Such a conflict is normal; it will happen in any school. But as can often happen, sometimes adults exacerbate rather than resolve a problem. In this case, when the student became defiant and was asked to go see the dean, the dean didn't deal with the issue very quickly, and the student was out of class for a very long time. In this video, as Hannah starts coaching her principal, she wants to improve both the quality of the dean's actions and the quality of the principal's coaching. What actions does Hannah take to push her principal's development in leading others to lead student culture?

 WATCH Clip 14: Lofthus—See It and Name It (Coach by Meeting)

Stop and Jot

What actions does Hannah take to push her principal's development in leading student culture?

_____

_____

_____

_____

What is extraordinary is just how much Hannah accomplishes in a very short time:

- **See the success.** Hannah starts by naming where the principal had succeeded in implementing previous feedback. This supports the principal's development as a culture leader by showing her what she's doing well—and setting her up to confidently take on the issue she and Hannah are going to address today.

- **Name the model.** Hannah asks her principal, "In a perfect world, what should it look like when a student is sent to the dean?" In other examples in this book, the manager has shown a model. In this case, the principal is clearly able to name what it should look like, which allows them to move on to the gap.

- **See the gap.** Hannah asks the classic gap question: "What is the gap between the model and your assistant principal's execution?" But she also asks, "What is the impact of not doing this?" This was invaluable for the leader to appreciate the negative impact of what occurred.

- **Name and punch the action step.** Finally, Hannah prompts her principal to name the action step based on their discussion. When applicable, this should include naming an action step for the teacher as well as for the leader. Work with the leader to confirm the quality of the action step: "Why is that highest leverage?" "Is that bite-size?"

Do It

Now it's time for Hannah and her principal to Do It: to practice the action steps they've identified. Take a look at the clip here to see how they do it. What actions does Hannah take to coach her principal to lead student culture?

 WATCH Clip 15: Lofthus—Do It (Coach by Meeting)

Stop and Jot

What actions does Hannah take to coach her principal to lead student culture?

_____

_____

_____

_____

Hannah follows the formula of every principal manager we've met thus far: she gets the principal to do it.

- **Plan.** To translate the practice as much as possible to mirror the principal's daily work, Hannah and her principal pick a real scenario to practice—in this case, the incident with the student who stole the lotion. They plan what each of their roles would be, with Hannah playing the role of the assistant principal who needs coaching.
- **Practice the gap.** With an effective plan in place, Hannah makes the practice effective by zeroing in on the gap that was most challenging: "What is highest-leverage [part to practice] based on your action step?" How you answer that question

can change the practice significantly. In this case, Hannah's principal is to practice giving real-time feedback so that she can support the assistant principal in getting students back into class as quickly as possible. From there, she and Hannah take it live.

- **Lock it in.** After a few rounds of practice, Hannah locks in what she and her principal have been practicing. Here, she brings it back to the action step: "Let's go back to our action step: Did we do every part of it?" That way, they make sure the principal leaves the meeting fully equipped to implement this action step herself once Hannah is no longer there.

Imagine what happens if every one of your check-ins has this quality of practice. Just as Juliana, LaKimbre, and Jesse did, Hannah is dramatically accelerating the growth of her principal and, in doing so, the school. And Hannah uses the same guide for her check-ins on Student Culture as what we introduced in Chapter 3 on Data-Driven Instruction. See It, Name it, Do it applies to all of the leadership levers.

	Principal Manager Check-In
	A Guide for Developing Principals One-on-One
Prepare	**Prepare**
	Plan your meeting:
	• (When possible) Do a pre-walkthrough of the school and/or look at the assessment data/student work so that you can plan your agenda.
	• Plan around goal from previous week.
	• Have available leader's current and upcoming plans: observation schedule, meeting scripts, PD plans.
	Have your tools in hand:
	• Universal:
	o Leverage Leadership Sequence of Action Steps for Principals
	o Content-specific one-pagers (e.g., Habits of Discussion, 5–12 Reading, etc.)
	• Data and planning:

Prepare	Prepare
	o Data dashboard and interim assessments
	o Weekly Data Meeting one-pager
	o Posted lesson plans with embedded feedback/reteach plans
	• Culture:
	o Student and Staff Culture Rubrics and Student Culture one-pager
	• Observation and feedback:
	o Get Better Faster Scope and Sequence and Coach's Guide
	o Observation Tracker and Giving Effective Feedback one-pager
See It	See It: Success, Model, and Gap

See the success:

• Look at recent data (student work, culture) and quickly ID progress and next steps.

  o "We set a goal of _____, and I noticed how you [met goal] by [concrete actions leader took]."

  o "What made that successful? What was the impact of [that positive action]?"

See the model:

• Narrow the focus: "Today, I want to dive into [one aspect of one of the leadership levers]."

• Name the exemplar.

  o "What should we see when we [observe the class, look at data, etc.]? What do you want the [class/routine/student work] to look like? What were your goals for [this teacher]?"

  o "Let's look at [exemplar rubric/upcoming student assessment]. What will teachers/students need to be able to do to demonstrate mastery?"

• (If unable to name the exemplar) Show a model—choose one:

  o Show video of effective leadership/teaching: "What do you notice about [model]? What are the key actions the [teacher/leader] takes that makes her effective?"

  o Model: "What do you notice about how I _____?" "What is the impact and purpose?"

See It	See It: Success, Model, and Gap
	o Provide real-time feedback in class: "When I intervened, what did I do? What was the impact?"
	o Read a one-pager or prompting guide: "What are the essential elements of _____?"
	See the gap:
	• Ask "What is the gap between [end goal/model] and what we saw today?"
	• Ask "What is causing the gap? What is the challenge in implementing this effectively?"
	• (If unable to name the gap) Present the evidence.
	o Present time-stamped video of leader: "What is the teacher/ student doing? What are you doing?" "What is the gap between what we see in this video and the [exemplar]?"
	o Present evidence: "The teacher is not writing anything down during your meeting. How does this impact the likelihood of her implementing your feedback?"
Name It	**Name It: High-Leverage, Measurable, Bite-Size Action Step**
	Name the action step:
	• (When applicable) For the *teacher/student*: "Based on what we discussed today, what do you think the action step for [teacher/ student work] should be?"
	• For the *leader*: "What do you think is your action step as a leader?"
	Punch it:
	• "Let's stamp it with precise language."
	• (When applicable) "So the teacher's action step is _____ [e.g., What to Do directions]."
	• "And your action step is _____."
	o *What* the leader will work on (e.g., plan before you practice during feedback meetings)
	o *How* the leader will execute (e.g., "1. Give them two minutes to prepare a script. 2. Review and revise the script. 3. Add additional scripting for anticipated challenges.")

Name It	Name It: High-Leverage, Measurable, Bite-Size Action Step
	o "In your own words, tell me your action step . . . Let's write that down."

Do It	Do It: Plan, Practice, Follow Up

Plan before practice:

- Script the changes into upcoming plans (for meetings or observations).
  - o "Where would be a good place and time to implement this next week?"
  - o "What are all the actions you need to take/want to see in the teachers?"
  - o "Take three minutes to write up your plan."
- Push to make the plan more precise and more detailed.
  - o "What prompts will you use with teachers that we can practice today?"
  - o "Now that you've made your initial plan, what will do you if [key challenge: e.g., resistant teacher]?"
- (If struggling to make a strong plan) Model for the leader and debrief.
  - o "Watch what I do and say as I model _____." "What do you notice about how I did _____?"
- Perfect the plan.
  - o "Those three steps look great. Let's add _____ to your [script/meeting plan]."

Practice:

- Round 1: "Let's practice" or "Let's take it live."
  - o (When applicable) Stand up/move around to simulate the whole-school leadership feeling.
  - o Pause the role play at the point of error to give immediate feedback.
  - o Repeat until the practice is successful.
- Additional rounds: master it while adding complexity.
  - o "Let's try that again, but this time I will be [teacher X who is slightly more challenging]."

Do It	Do It: Plan, Practice, Follow Up
	• (Once mastered) Lock it in.
	o "Let's look back at our action step. Did we master each part of it?"
	o "Let's reflect on this role play. What made you successful? Why is that important?"
	Follow up:
	• Name the tasks: both leader and supervisor write down all tasks with deadlines.
	o Completed materials: when leader will complete revised plans/materials
	o Manager observation: when you'll observe the leader
	o (When valuable) Leader observation of master teacher/leader: when she'll observe master teacher/leader live or via video implementing the action step
	o (When valuable) Self-video: when you'll video leader to debrief in future meeting
	• Set the dates.
	o "When would be the best time to observe your implementation of this?" *or* "When I review your plans, I'll look for this modification."
	o Newer leader: "I'll come in [later this week] and look for [evidence of change]."
Plan Time	**Plan the Use of Time**
	Plan leader's schedule for upcoming weeks:
	• "Based on your successes and challenges this week, how would you adjust your weekly plan?"
	• "Based on today's check-in and your new action step, let's adjust your weekly plan."
	• "Where will this be difficult to follow? How can you set yourself up for success?"

Hannah and Jesse show us how to maximize your time spent with your principals. But even if you maximize the time, you still cannot be there every day. More than

90 percent of the time, leaders have to drive student culture on their own. How can you influence that 90 percent when you are not there?

THE 30-DAY PLAYBOOK

Hannah's impact will be lasting only if the action steps she delivers become habit. Practice helps lock in that habit significantly. Yet some leaders will still struggle when she's not by their side. How can managers get their principals to the point where great cultural leadership is habitual?

Take a cue from Bill Walsh, one of the most successful professional football coaches of all time. One of Walsh's many legacies was the way he called plays for his offense. At the time Walsh was coaching in 1980, every coach made a decision in the moment of which play his offense should run. This would happen roughly sixty-five times a game. Each team had hundreds of plays to choose from, and each coach needed to decide within a few seconds.

At one point, Walsh realized that he wasn't at his best when trying to make decisions this way. So one night he decided to script the first seven plays of the game. No matter what the defense did, he told himself, he would stick with those plays.

Walsh's strategy worked. The team looked better, advanced the ball further, and had more success in those first plays than later. Walsh kept expanding the number of scripted plays until he reached thirty, or the equivalent of the entire first half. And his teams were wildly successful on offense.

In many ways, leading student culture is like coaching a football team. There are at least sixty moments in a day when a leader has to decide rapidly what she is going to do: what to say during breakfast, how to talk to a student who's upset or angry in the hallway, whether to restart a routine or not, and so forth. To help leaders who weren't instinctually good at leading culture, we have experimented with our own version of Walsh's success. Rather than a thirty-play script, we established what we call the 30-Day Playbook. Given that the first thirty days are essential to establishing culture, we encouraged leaders to make a minute-by-minute script showing what they would do throughout those first thirty days to set the right habits in place.

For new principals in particular, using a playbook gives them a remarkable ability to do what they otherwise wouldn't be able to without much more experience. One of Jesse's principals, Christine Algozo, wholeheartedly concurs:

> Sustaining strong student culture has been a key area of my own growth as
> a principal, and the 30-Day Playbook was a significant game-changer for

me. For the first time, I had a game plan for everything I and my leadership team needed to do. It freed my mind from overthinking and allowed me to focus on simply acting: taking the steps that would build the culture, one action at a time. By the end of thirty days, we had in place the strongest culture we've ever had, despite being larger than ever and with new leadership team members. It built habits that made it easy to sustain what we had worked so hard to establish.

As a resource for you, we have included on the DVD the complete 30-Day Playbook that Christine and Jesse used in their leadership of high school student culture. The key to an effective playbook is to make it your own: cut everything that doesn't work for you and adjust it to match your own context and vision. One easy way to make this work at your schools is to give your principal a copy of Jesse's 30-Day Playbook and prompt her to adjust it to meet her needs. Here's an excerpt of what that playbook looks like.

The 30-Day Playbook: High School Version

Between 7:40 a.m. and 7:58 a.m.: Student Breakfast

- **Student Culture Observation—Breakfast**
  - Observe student behavior at breakfast and note gaps in teacher presence or teacher actions
  - If needed, pull aside a student who is not following the norms: model for teachers a quiet correction

What to Scan for and Fix

- Staff not present in the lunchroom, not seen looking
- Students too loud or shouting
- Students blocking the entrance to the cafeteria or going to different rooms without approval
- Students standing, wandering
- Students leaving without permission or pass

- **Real-Time Coaching**
  - Note any teachers not coaching students for 100% behavior. Real-time coach using whisper prompts and/or modeling if necessary
  - Debrief quickly: "What did you notice me do? Why did I do that? What was the impact?"

- **Public Leadership Moment**
  - With 5 minutes remaining in breakfast, model the hand-raise procedure with all students; expect 100% of hands raised and silent within 3 seconds. Use *Do It Again* technique until success is achieved
  - Give public, precise praise to key students to build positive culture. Clearly state the expectations

- **Cue the Transition**
  - Restate the expectations for hallway transitions and let students know that staff will be watching them to ensure success:
    - Moving with purpose, not lingering in the hallway
    - Talking quietly, no shouting
    - Lining up at classroom doors (grades 9/10) or entering quietly (grades 11/12)

Stop and Jot

Identify the leaders you work with who would benefit from part or all of a playbook. What are the key habits you need to reinforce with them to build their skills? Identify the key components of a playbook you will implement with them to reinforce those habits.

_____

_____

_____

_____

How could you adjust this sample playbook to meet the needs of your own schools?

_____

_____

_____

_____

Like any leadership tool, the playbook has no value unless it's used. The best way to hold your principals accountable for the high-leverage actions captured in the playbook is to have them show you their used playbook each time you meet with them (either by scanning it or by bringing you their used copy of the playbook). The core questions you can ask leaders during every check-in to help them build the habits of leading a superb student culture are: "What worked about your playbook? What didn't?" "What do we have to change about how you're using your time this week?"

CONCLUSION

Hannah Lofthus is a creature of habit. Every week, she takes stock of where her schools are and where they need her support. She relentlessly monitors her student culture and coaches her principals to close the gaps. What's remarkable about her habits is that they are utterly replicable. To quote Aristotle, excellence is not a virtue but a habit. Build the habit of leading student culture, and excellence will follow.

Core Idea

Excellence is not a virtue but a habit.
Build the habit of leading student culture, and excellence will follow.

Leverage Leadership Sequence of Action Steps for Principals
Student Culture

Lever	Key Actions in Sequence
	PLAN
Student Culture	**Set the Vision**
	1. **Define your vision for student culture:**
	• See a model.
	o Review videos of implementation (e.g., from *Get Better Faster, Leverage Leadership, Teach Like a Champion*) and/ or visit high-performing schools or classrooms.
	o Record what teachers, leaders, and students say and do.

LEVER	KEY ACTIONS IN SEQUENCE
	PLAN

<table>
<tr><td rowspan="2" style="vertical-align:middle">STUDENT CULTURE</td><td>

- Define the model for your own school's routines and procedures.

  o Write what the leaders, teachers, and students should be doing.

  o Enumerate what will happen if a student doesn't follow directions.

  o Create a school-wide culture rubric that defines the following:

  - Common language that teachers and leaders will use

  - Vision for all school-wide and classroom routines and systems

- Anticipate the gap.

  o Determine what it would look like if student culture was executed poorly.

  o What would ineffective leaders and teachers be doing?

  o What would the students be doing if it was implemented poorly?

2. **Name It—build a minute-by-minute plan for every routine, procedure, and all-school culture moment:**

- Craft minute-by-minute systems for routines and procedures.

  o Name what leaders, students, and teachers will do in a comprehensive, sequential, minute-by-minute plan.

  - Describe every part of the day: arrival/breakfast, hallway transitions, in-class routines (including first and last 5 min of class), lunch, dismissal.

  - Include what will happen when students do not follow directions.

- Set goals and deadlines.

  o Set a concrete, measurable goal—e.g., hallway transitions will reduce to 1 min; increase all hands raised to 100%.

  o ID when the system will be *introduced* and when the goal will be *met*.

</td></tr>
</table>

Lever	Key Actions in Sequence
Student Culture	Plan

- o Determine the tool for measurement (e.g., Student Culture Rubric).

3. **Name It—build systems to manage student discipline (asst. principal, dean of students, etc.):**
   - Set up effective systems and routines for the leader who will drive student culture.
   - Set a weekly and daily schedule for that leader.
   - Create a clear protocol for responding to specific student discipline situations.
   - Build a standing agenda for principal–culture leader check-ins that includes:
     - o Data review of student discipline issues and most pressing student issues
     - o Feedback to the leader and to teachers who need support
     - o Review of send-out or suspension data to problem-solve ways to prevent the behavior

Roll Out

4. **Plan the rollout/rehearsal:**
   - Plan the rollout.
     - o Script a hook:
       - ▪ Frontload school values/mission—short and sweet speech that states rationale and purpose.
     - o Script the model.
       - ▪ Using clear and concise language, tell them the procedure and the sequence of the procedure. Everyone needs to know what it will look like.
       - ▪ Script what you will narrate as you model to highlight key takeaways.
     - o Plan the staff practice of the routine/procedure.
       - ▪ Script what you will say and do and script what teachers will say and do (roles, timing, etc.).

LEVER	KEY ACTIONS IN SEQUENCE
	ROLL OUT

<table>
<tr><td rowspan="30">STUDENT CULTURE</td><td>

■ Script what real-time feedback you will give during practice, with associated prompts.

5. **Roll out/rehearse:**

- See It—model the routine/procedure.

  o Hook: deliver a hook (short and sweet) that gives them the "why."

  o Frame: name what you want them to observe: "As you watch the model of [routine/procedure], I want you to be thinking about . . ."

  o Model: exaggerate the model to reinforce every action you want to see.

- Name It—debrief the model.

  o Ask "What did you notice? Teacher actions? Student actions?"

  o Narrate the why: "Why is that [action] important?"

  o Reflect: "Jot down your key takeaways before we jump into practice."

- Do It—practice the routine/procedure.

  o Give clear What to Do directions:

    ■ What the main participant will do (time for her to plan/script her actions)

    ■ What the audience will do (cue cards, preprepared student roles)

  o Round 1—practice the basic routine and procedure from start to finish.

    ■ Give feedback at the point of error and have them do it again.

  o Round 2 (after teachers have built muscle memory)—add complexity (e.g., student misbehavior, student learning errors).

  o Lock it in and rename the action plan:

</td></tr>
</table>

LEVER	KEY ACTIONS IN SEQUENCE

	ROLL OUT

- "How did what we practice meet or enhance the action plan we named?"

	EXECUTE

STUDENT CULTURE

6. **Lead publicly:**
   - Be present and be seen in key areas (lunch, hallways, struggling classrooms, etc.).
   - Communicate urgency (verbal and nonverbal).
     - o Nonverbal: point to students who need redirecting; move students along.
     - o Verbal: Do It Again until 100%; challenge ("First period did this. Can you do it, too?").
   - Provide immediate feedback.
     - o Model concrete phrases and actions that teachers should use (keep it succinct).
     - o Address student noncompliance on the spot; follow up face-to-face with teacher.
     - o Use precise praise and celebrate success (individual and team) verbally and via email.

7. **Manage individually:**
   - Teachers—have "course correction" conversations when they are struggling.
     - o ID the challenge.
     - o State the impact.
     - o Make bite-size action plan with prompt implementation on a set timeline.
   - Leaders—implement check-in with the leader in charge of student discipline issues (AP/dean).
     - o Model effective student de-escalation and reflection techniques for the AP/dean and have AP/dean execute.
     - o Monitor and give AP/dean real-time feedback to ensure AP/dean meets current action step.

Lever	Key Actions in Sequence
	Execute

Student Culture	• Students—lead effective discipline conversations by following the model.
	
	  o Listen: ask them to explain their version of what happened.
	
	  o Name the problem and then the consequence.
	
	  o Share why this is important (back to shared mission and long-term dreams for the child).
	
	  o End with shared commitment to work together.
	
	• Families—lead effective discipline conversations with families.
	
	  o Name the problem and then the consequence.
	
	  o Listen: acknowledge their feelings and their concerns ("open face," eye contact, emotional constancy).
	
	  o Economy of language: keep language concise and precise, and stick to the script.

	Monitor and Course-Correct

	8. **Measure student culture and ID the gaps:**
	
	• Via a school walkthrough, ID students and teachers not implementing routines effectively and ID the action steps.
	
	  o With Student Culture Rubric in hand, ID where the breakdown occurs:
	
	    ▪ What student actions or inactions are indicators of the problem?
	
	    ▪ What teacher actions or inactions are causing the problem?
	
	    ▪ What leader actions or inactions are causing the problem?
	
	  o Bring people outside your leadership team to observe your school and ID the big rocks to move your school culture forward.
	
	• Targeted improvements: choose one row on the student culture rubric and set a specific goal for a score by a specific

LEVER	KEY ACTIONS IN SEQUENCE
	MONITOR AND COURSE-CORRECT
STUDENT CULTURE	date. Develop clear action steps and implement. Rescore that row on a regular basis. 9. **Lead a whole-school reset of a specific, high-leverage routine/procedure:** • Revisit the model: what the routine should look like. • See the gap: have teachers/leaders ID the gaps. • Model the reset (follow the actions in the rollout section). • Execute a daily walkthrough to monitor the targeted action steps. • Communicate to staff the progress and next steps on a daily basis until the goal is met.

Pulling the Lever: Action Planning Worksheet

Coaching Principals on Student Culture

Schools Assessment

• What are the biggest gaps in your vision for student culture and what you see in each of your schools? (Remember: use a rubric to make it measurable)

_____

_____

_____

Leader Assessment

• Which of the actions from the Leverage Leadership Sequence of Action Steps for Principals do you want to target this year as you develop your principals?

_____

_____

_____

Planning for Action

- What tools from this book will you use to lead your schools? Check all that you will use. (All are available on the DVD unless noted otherwise.)

  ☐ Student Culture one-pager

  ☐ Principal Manager Check-In one-pager

  ☐ Student Culture Rubric

  ☐ 30-Day Playbook

  ☐ PD on student culture for principal managers

  ☐ PD on student culture for principals (see *Leverage Leadership 2.0*)

  ☐ Network and school data dashboard samples

  ☐ Other: _____

- How will you modify these resources to meet your district's needs?

  _____

  _____

  _____

- What are your next steps for coaching principals around student culture?

Action	Date

Chapter 5

Coaching Teams of Principals

Stronger Together

It's 3:00 p.m., and this team of principals is just getting started. They're not scattered at their individual schools but gathered together at Annie Webb Blanton Elementary School, home of Laura Garza. They are huddled in groups of four, all of them hooked into a laptop of one of their peers.

"As you watch this video of a weekly data meeting, pull out your feedback cheat sheet: What are the strengths, and what are the two highest-leverage action steps I could offer my peer to improve?" says their district leader, Teresa Khirallah. As Teresa finishes delivering these instructions, the first principal in each group has his or her video teed up and ready to watch. "Let's get stronger together," says Teresa. "Ready? You may begin."

After each principal has taken a moment to set the context for his or her video, voices in the classroom fall silent as each group watches a video of one of their peers delivering feedback to a teacher. Every principal is scribbling notes in his or her handout, observing . . . and learning.

Teresa Khirallah, program officer at the Teaching Trust, a highly successful principal training program in Texas, has had an outsized impact on education. Her results across multiple schools are among the greatest successes in school management in the entire country.

72%
of schools led by
Teaching Trust leaders
are closing the gap
faster than peer schools

86%
of schools led by Teaching
Trust Leadership Teams
are closing the gap faster
than peer schools

2.5x
the expected number of
Teaching Trust–led schools are
in the **top 10%** highest-growth
schools (26% of schools)

2x
the expected number of
Teaching Trust–led schools are
in the **top 25%** highest-growth
schools (48% of schools)

Source: Boston Consulting Group analysis of TEA STAAR 2013–2016 math and reading data at the postsecondary readiness level

(You can read more about a few of the principals she has impacted in *Leverage Leadership 2.0.*)

Teresa didn't start that way. In fact, when she first transitioned from serving as a principal to training leaders, she didn't have that much success. She would lead PD or meet with a principal, but nothing changed. "I felt like I told them what to do," Teresa recalls, "but it didn't stick when they left the meeting." Teresa felt that she was spread so thin across so many leaders that she couldn't figure out a way to give them enough time to get better.

Teresa's transformation began when she identified the root cause: she wasn't giving her principals sufficient time to practice. First, she had to confront her assumption that principals didn't need practice; only teachers did. This assumption is endemic in the professional world—the higher you rise in an organization, the less professional development you require. Yet the opposite is true: the bigger the leadership role you hold, the more complex the work you do, and the more support you need.

Core Idea

The higher you rise, the less PD you receive.
Yet the bigger the leadership role, the more practice you need.

In the previous chapters, we saw how you can coach a principal one-on-one and make practice the priority, immediately changing outcomes. But with only so many hours in a day, how do you increase the "at-bats" for each principal? The quick answer: leverage your team.

Being a principal can be profoundly isolating. When you are in your school building, everyone looks to you to lead—but few are there to support you. Even when a principal manager coaches a principal every week, that still leaves significant time unsupported. The way to change this is to give the principal a true team to be a part of—not as the leader but as a peer. How? Form a team of principals.

Core Idea

Increase your leverage by leveraging the team.

What does it look like to form a true team of principals who care as much for their peers' results as for their own? Read on, and you'll see how Teresa and other principal managers make that happen.

ESTABLISH THE NORM—ONE SCHOOL

Before becoming a leader of leaders, Nikki Bridges led Leadership Prep Ocean Hill (LPOH) in Brooklyn, New York, to incredible heights. LPOH's students hail from the neighborhood of Brownsville, which has historically been one of the most impoverished communities in the United States, and 99 percent of them come from racial minority groups.[1] Yet these children consistently outperform their peers not only throughout their city but throughout their state, with test scores that place them in the top 2 percent of achievers in both math and ELA. How did Nikki get—and keep—her school in such a position?

Nikki calls the key to her success "the 5 percent rule." "If classrooms on a grade team are not within 5 percentage points of one another, then something is wrong," Nikki states. Such a disparity would mean that one teacher has figured out a more effective method for teaching and hasn't shared it completely with his or her grade-level team. "We shouldn't be competing with one another. One school."

"One school" is a powerful mantra: it suggests that being successful on my own is actually harmful, not helpful. It suggests that just having the students in my classroom or school succeed more than others means we are not as invested in other children. As soon as we reach out beyond the walls of our classroom or school, we communicate that each child matters.

"One school" is what enabled Nikki's fourth-grade team to push each other and get better collectively. In the end, it was what contributed to consistently strong results. "I don't shy away from saying we're all going to use a best practice," says Nikki. "For example, when one grade-level team started tracking data and it was yielding results for the team, all classrooms adopted the system. When someone found a way to make the system more efficient, we let them test it out. It worked. We adopted it across the school." Nikki uses this virtuous cycle to align norms at all the schools she leads. This ensures that all her leaders, all her teachers, and all her students succeed. At Nikki's school, you didn't have to advocate for the best teacher for your child; you knew that any classroom would suffice.

"One school" is also a mantra that principals can share with one another. If your children are as important and valuable as mine, why wouldn't I support you to be the best version of yourself?

Core Idea

Invite your principals to be "one school" with each other.
Then set the norms to make that happen.

Once you've named a norm you need structures that make that norm a habit. Nikki and Teresa both swear by two key strategies:

- Observe each other to give and get feedback.
- Practice together.

Essentially, you are creating a culture of feedback and practice. Why do these two strategies work so effectively? Read on.

OBSERVE EACH OTHER—COLLABORATIVE SCHOOL WALKTHROUGHS

Stronger Together—Walkthroughs

Five principals are gathered in the office of Tildi Sharp, principal of Lincoln Park High School. An LCD projector is attached to the computer of assistant superintendent Jesse Corburn. Displayed on the wall are all the accolades that Tildi's principal peers just shared after spending two hours walking around and observing her school. These accolades praise one of Tildi's strongest teachers ("She is an exemplar for the rest of us on her monitoring and pacing") and champion the quality of lesson plans, What to Do directions, and Tildi's real-time feedback across the campus. Tildi has just finished sharing what she was most proud of about these strengths.

"Congratulations on these commendations, Tildi," affirms Jesse. "Now let's shift our conversation to areas for growth: What are the highest-leverage action steps you would recommend to Tildi to improve the school? We'll go around the room twice. You can propose a new action step or build off of the recommendation of your colleague. Thomas, can you start us off?"

Thomas O'Brien, Tildi's principal peer, looks through his consolidated notes and shares, "My highest-leverage action step would be to lead a PD on monitoring student work to collect data." He shares his evidence that while teachers were walking around the classroom looking at student work, they weren't collecting data to respond to student error.

"That was my top action step as well," shares Erica Lim, a principal fellow. "And I would add on . . ."

When most educators talk about school walkthroughs, they refer to moments when the principal walks the school with her leadership team, or a superintendent walks the school with the principal. These are helpful but limited, because the principal doesn't learn from anyone other than his or her manager. The power of the walkthrough changes when principals learn as part of a team.

The Impact of Peer Walkthroughs

Let's contemplate the impact of the walkthrough of Lincoln Park High School that opened this section. Five high school principals and principal fellows have formed a team; all of them visit one another's schools twice a year to do a walkthrough and give feedback. Think of the domino effect of this one walkthrough:

- **Set fresh eyes on the school.** When a principal is in his own school every day, he can stop seeing the weak spots on campus. A particular low-performing classroom becomes a normal sight, and a sense of the urgency of bringing that classroom up to speed decreases. Peers bring fresh eyes. "When peer principals are visiting my school, I find myself seeing the school in a new light," comments principal Tildi Sharp. "I see it as an outsider would see it, which gives me newfound urgency to tackle the problems."

- **See the exemplar.** The power of the walkthrough is not just to find the areas for growth; it is also to see the exemplar in action. Julia Addeo is the Algebra II teacher at Tildi's school, and she has the strongest interim assessment scores in the entire high school network. When Tildi's peers came to observe her school, they weren't just giving her feedback. They were getting the opportunity to see the exemplar teacher in action—and to bring those best practices back to their own schools.

- **Sharpen action planning and follow-up.** A major struggle for many school leaders is to determine concrete action steps. We can spot a problem—that's what we're good at! Trying to fix it is another thing. Going on a walkthrough of someone else's school gives leaders practice at sharpening their action steps and being more concrete. Multiple principals walk away with the same action plan for their own school.

- **Peer support—and accountability.** All of these strengths lead to one huge outcome: principals start to lean on each other. They get comfortable asking each other for feedback, and they don't want to let each other down. "When I know my peers are coming back in three months to see my school again," Tildi shares, "I have a real desire to show them how I've implemented their feedback. I don't want to let them down."

Patrick Lencioni is one of the leading authors on what makes leadership teams highly effective. In his seminal text *The Five Dysfunctions of a Team,* he highlights a key quality that distinguishes high-achieving teams from the rest: team members don't want to let each other down.[2] That is a difficult trait to teach, but peer walkthroughs can be a powerful step in the right direction. When principals want their teammates to succeed, they push each other to new heights.

How to Run a Peer Walkthrough

For you to get these walkthroughs in place, your core role as a principal manager is simply to organize and facilitate. Here is a simple agenda to make walkthroughs happen:

- **Observe for a few hours—both the floor and the ceiling.** A few hours is enough time for a group of leaders to see what they need to in a school and also to have time left for what comes next: feedback and action planning. Make sure that you see the top teachers (start from the exemplar!) and the most struggling teachers, and this will give the team the opportunity to close the gaps between the two.

- **Use a monitoring tool.** When you are doing peer walkthroughs for the first time, you are also establishing a common framework and language. The easiest way to do that is to use a common rubric or checklist. As Jesse Corburn will tell you, having that tool in hand is the easiest way to see gaps clearly. Using a rubric can also enable the principal to walk away with an objective measure of his school in addition to the concrete feedback.

- **Share out accolades.** When the time comes for leaders to share what they have seen, what works well in one-on-one feedback meetings will also work well in a group: start with praise. In addition to being constructive for the person receiving feedback, this gives leaders an opportunity to identify practices they may wish to replicate at their schools.

- **Narrow down to two to three top areas for growth.** What's true for feedback meetings is true during walkthroughs: fewer action steps are more. Narrow the conversation to the two or three things the leader needs to do *most* urgently to improve learning at her campus.

- **Make an action plan.** If the leader whose campus you've just walked through isn't left with a plan to implement the feedback you and the other leaders you work with have provided, that feedback is all too likely to slip through the cracks.

Here is the protocol that Jesse uses with his principal team.

Stop and Jot

How could you implement or improve the quality of peer walkthroughs for your principal team?

_____

_____

_____

_____

_____

Peer Walkthrough Protocol

Uncommon Schools

Total Walkthrough Time: 2 hr, 45 min

Time	Length	Task
Introduction		
9:00	15 min	**Arrival and walkthrough overview** • Set parameters for the walkthrough. • Share the rubric/tool. • Pass out schedules.
Observations		
9:15	90 min	**Classroom observations**
Team Debrief		
10:45	15 min	**Individual reflection** • Consolidate notes. • Evaluate school on the rubric. • Identify commendations and top action steps.
11:00	5 min	**Sharing of rubric scores**
11:05	10 min	**Praise** • Round robin: each leader shares highest commendations (go around twice).
11:15	15 min	**Action steps** • Round robin: each leader shares highest-leverage action step to improve the school. • Subsequent leaders can either build off of the previous action steps or add a new one. • If there are many different action steps, principal manager pushes the group to identify the highest-leverage ones and to narrow the focus.

Time	Length	Task

11:30	15 min	**Action planning**
		
		• Host principal utilizes last 15 min to react to the action steps and get advice on building an action plan.
		
		• Depending on the action steps, the action planning could include:
		
		  o Developing an agenda for a PD for teachers
		
		  o Developing an agenda for the school leadership team meeting
		
		  o Designing a whole-school reset of a culture routine

Peer walkthroughs are a huge step toward a "one school" culture. The real magic starts to happen when you combine them with opportunities to practice together. Let's see how.

PRACTICE TOGETHER—TEAM COACHING

Here is a powerful question to ask yourself when assessing the quality of the meetings you have with your principals as a team: How much of the time that principals spend in meetings together is devoted to practicing instructional leadership?

If your answer is little to none, join the club! Most principal managers share the same answer. Too often when principals are removed from their schools, they sit in meetings where they listen a lot, but practice little. Changing this culture means remembering the core idea about leading professional development: your principal team meetings are only as powerful as what you practice.

Core Idea

Just like PD, your principal team meetings are only as powerful as what you practice.

Two takeaways are implied here:

• *Every* meeting with a team of principals should be considered an opportunity for professional development, which means time for practice.

- Any meeting with a team of principals that does not involve practice should be limited or eliminated.

These are provocative statements, but they shouldn't be ignored. It's no exaggeration to say that those actions are at the heart of changing the way we work with principals. Stop talking *at* them and start practicing *with* them.

> ## Core Idea
> Stop talking *at* principals and start practicing *with* them.

To do that, you can use the framework for leading professional development (PD) from *Leverage Leadership 2.0*. Let's see what that looks like for principals and instructional leaders.

What to Practice: The Seven Levers

PD matters when it responds to a need and when it changes outcomes. There is no better place to start with principals than aligning to the leadership levers. *Driven by Data, Leverage Leadership 2.0*, and *Get Better Faster* include training materials for nearly every leadership lever:

- Data-Driven Instruction 101: *Driven by Data*
- Data-Driven Instruction 201—Weekly Data Meetings: *Get Better Faster*
- Observation and Feedback 101: *Leverage Leadership 2.0*
- Observation and Feedback 201—Real-Time Feedback: *Get Better Faster*
- Professional Development: *Leverage Leadership 2.0*
- Student Culture: *Leverage Leadership 2.0*

Pick one lever at a time and start developing your principals together. To give you a sense of what that looks like, the following sections break down how principal managers lead PD for other principals and instructional leaders.

See It and Name it

To restate a core idea from *Leverage Leadership 2.0*: if you want people to get it, get them to see it.

> ## Core Idea
>
> If you want people to get it, get them to see it.

This is just as true for principals as it is for teachers. For principals to be able to practice effectively, they need to know what exemplary instructional leadership looks like.

Take a look at this video of Teresa Khirallah launching a feedback meeting with a leadership team in Dallas.

WATCH Clip 16: Khirallah—See It and Name It—Leading Leadership Teams

---

Stop and Jot

What does Teresa do to launch her PD? Jot down what you noticed.

_____

_____

_____

_____

_____

_____

_____

When you watch the discussion, it's clear why this strategy works: seeing is believing. Leaders see the impact of effective feedback, and the core idea comes to life before their eyes.

Remember the keys to making this work:

- **Choose a strong model.** Either take a clip directly from one of the books listed earlier, or film one of your top instructional leaders. There is power in leaders seeing one of their peers as a model, so this can add value!

- **Keep it short.** A long video or model won't hold participants' attention—and will take valuable time away from practicing. So keep it short: no longer than five minutes.

- **Make the focus specific.** Give participants targeted questions on what they should be looking for in the model.

- **Punch it.** Once the participants generate all of the most essential cognitive work, punch the core idea with formal language. Even at this point, keep your language succinct and precise—think three to five bullets or a core idea that makes it shine.

Bill Graham is a communications expert: he devotes himself to training some of the most influential people to motivate and influence others. By following these steps, we've put his most famous advice into action: make the complicated simple, and the simple powerful.

Core Idea

"Make the complicated simple and the simple powerful."

—Bill Graham

Do It

If your PD is only as powerful as your practice, then your See It and Name It are only valuable in making your practice effective. Getting principals to practice together is powerful:

- They strengthen their leadership skills.

- They get used to giving and getting feedback on instructional leadership.

- They see that everyone is being held to the same bar, which is a powerful motivator and makes them feel part of a team rather than alone!

Watch an example of the power of practice among principals in action:

 WATCH Clip 17: Corburn—Do It (Plan)—Leading PD

What actions does Jesse take to make his teachers better? Jot down what you noticed.

_____

_____

_____

_____

_____

_____

_____

This is where we see Teresa's wisdom about letting her principals practice together come into play most unmistakably. The heart of the PD is when leaders get out of their chairs and learn from each other. Let's unpack what the leaders in this video do to make their practice—and their entire PD—powerful.

Anyone who's ever stood up to rehearse a set of actions can testify that if you haven't thought ahead, you freeze up on the spot. Jesse anticipates this challenge by giving his participants the opportunity to plan before they practice. That sets everyone up to practice perfectly.

Core Idea

The precision of your plan determines the quality of your practice.
Perfect the plan before you practice.

Jesse took the following key step to make the practice effective:

- **Use your tools to script it.** Use your one-pagers on instructional leadership to guide the planning: principals don't need to reinvent the wheel! That way, Jesse knows that when principals stand up to practice, they'll already have their first moves down.

Once you've planned it, you can practice. Watch how Kelly leads the practice.

- **Deliver clear instructions.** Kelly has simple, clear instructions. That can make the difference between chaos and targeted, all-in practice.

- **Practice the gap.** Focus the practice on what principals need the most—is that the See It? The Do It? Or some other aspect of leadership? Practice only matters if it closes a leadership gap.

- **Get feedback and do it again.** The goal of the PD is not simply to experience practice: it is to practice perfectly! Kelly therefore makes sure each participant has a chance to do it again to incorporate the feedback and get even better.

See It. Name It. Do It. Reflect. When you have these steps in place, PD can produce powerful instructional leadership.

CONCLUSION

Ask Teresa what she values most about her work as a leader of leaders, and she's quick to respond: "There's been something incredibly magical about connecting people to a movement," she says. Under her leadership, it's not just individual schools that grow; instead, leaders learn from one another. In doing so, they become part of a wave of leaders across the globe who not only *wish* to serve children better but do so; and not only their own students but the students their peers are leading as well.

Leaders like Teresa, like her principals, and like all of us have one thing in common: we cannot do this work alone. To break away from the "Superman" narrative of touching our students' lives, we must lean on one another. The greatest leaders of all are those who make that possible at every chance they have.

Pulling the Lever: Action Planning Worksheet
Coaching Principals as a Team

Planning for Action

- What tools from this chapter will you use to lead your schools? Check all that you will use.
  - ☐ Peer Walkthrough Protocol (DVD)
  - ☐ PD Session Plans and Materials (DVD)
    - ☐ Data-Driven Instruction 101 (*Driven by Data*)

☐ Data-Driven Instruction 201—Weekly Data Meetings (*Get Better Faster*)

☐ Observation and Feedback 101 (*Leverage Leadership 2.0*)

☐ Observation and Feedback 201—Real-Time Feedback (*Get Better Faster*)

☐ Professional Development (*Leverage Leadership 2.0*)

☐ Student Culture (*Leverage Leadership 2.0*)

☐ Other: _____

- How will you modify these resources to meet your district's needs?

  _____

  _____

  _____

- What are your next steps for coaching your principals as a team?

Action	Date

Part 3

Systems

Chapter 6

Finding the Time

Putting It All Together

Before assistant superintendent Serena Savarirayan finishes her weekly check-in with principal Eric Diamon, they take stock of everything they have worked on and put it on their calendars. They've identified the key gaps, particularly in seventh-grade math, that Eric and his team will need to close to keep every student on track, and they've practiced reteaching those gaps.

"Can we roll out these reteaches this week?" Eric asks.

Serena nods in affirmation: "This should fit right into the lesson plans you have scheduled for this," she says, pointing out the opportune moments for teachers to reteach this content. Then she turns to her calendar. "When I come back next week, we can co-observe that grade, so we'll be able to see how students are doing with this material."

Eric nods, and they both update their calendars and action plans. Serena's action plan is already full of notes from each of her principal check-ins, clearly highlighting her area of focus for each school. She adds her notes about Eric's reteach plans.

"You know, Tonya and Vernon [peer principals] are working on the same actions. We'll make this the focus of our principal team meeting next Wednesday."

"Great!" responds Eric. "Do you have their action plans so I can use them to strengthen my own?"

"Sure," says Serena, as she pulls up the action plans from her last check-in.

Let's be honest: every role in a school is hard—from teaching to leading. Assistant superintendent Serena Savarirayan recalls the challenge of each new role: "I remember how hard it was in my first years of teaching, and that continued in my first years of being a principal. And being an assistant superintendent? It felt like none of my teaching and principal experience prepared me for that challenge."

Managing multiple schools is hard—extremely so. Yet Serena didn't let that get in the way of success. To that point, all of the middle schools that Serena manages in Newark, New Jersey, are among the highest performing in the state, far exceeding the statewide average and even the proficiency of the highest-income students in the state (see Figure 6.1).

Figure 6.1 New Jersey PARCC Assessment: North Star Academy Middle Schools, Percentage at or Above Proficiency in Algebra I (top) and Eighth-Grade ELA (bottom), 2017

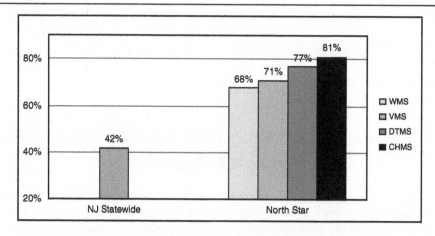

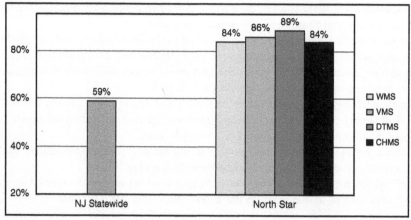

Somehow, amid all the challenges of being principal manager, Serena found a way to lead schools effectively—so effectively that there is little gap in achievement among her schools. How? She clearly leveraged data-driven instruction and student culture, as we saw from her peers in previous chapters. And she did so by becoming the master of her own time.

As a principal manager, you no doubt find that all too many challenges are beyond your control—from state or national mandates to local events that impact your schools' community. Your time probably feels like one of those uncontrollable factors, but in reality, it's the one thing you *can* control.

Core Idea

Leading schools probably makes you feel as if don't have control of your time, but in reality, it's the one thing you *can* control.

The previous chapters in this book showed what to do to drive learning in every school you manage. This one will show you how to find the time to do it—not in a rigid way, but in a way that lets you adapt to the needs of your schools and leaves you enough extra hours to manage curveballs as they come. Following the scheduling process outlined in this chapter will let you lock in the instructional and cultural work that will best serve your schools, and lock out almost everything else.

Core Idea

By intentionally planning the use of your time, you can lock in instructional and cultural leadership—and lock out almost everything else.

Let's dive in.

BUILD YOUR WEEKLY SCHEDULE

When you look at a leader's schedule, you'll see her priorities. The opening scene between Serena and her principal Eric Diamon could never have taken place if Serena hadn't created a calendar with time specifically blocked out for meetings like those. For Serena, finding the time is a matter not of fruitlessly scrambling to add more hours to the day but of building her schedule from the start around the instructional actions that matter most.

Now it's your turn to do the same! We'll walk through the steps Serena takes to build her schedule so that you can follow along to build yours as well. As an overview, here's the process we're about to undertake:

1. Prework—distribute your teachers across your leadership team.
2. Block out external/district commitments.
3. Lock in instructional meetings.
4. Lock in other instructional activities.
5. Lock in work time for big projects.

What does this look like? Let's walk through it piece by piece.

(If you're able to do so, print out the provided Weekly Schedule Template—which you'll also find in the DVD—and fill it in as you read!)

Prework: Get to a 6:1—or 12:1—Ratio

The number one variable that will influence your schedule is the number of principals you will manage directly. For weekly principal check-ins of two to three hours each (which is the time it will take to do the sort of check-ins you've seen from the leaders in this book), the golden ratio is 6:1. For biweekly check-ins, the ratio is 12:1. Thus, if you manage twelve or fewer principals, you can skip this prework and go right to Step 2!

If you manage more than twelve principals, you'll want to find some help. Where? From your own team.

In nearly every district that is large enough to have principal managers in charge of more than twelve schools each, there are additional central office staff devoted to the coaching of the principals. In some cases, a principal manager has a deputy. In other cases, there are literacy and math coaches and other supports, often working alongside but not in coordination with the principal manager. Rethinking those relationships can significantly enhance your impact. This is rooted in the same point we've made about instructional leadership at the school level: a teacher benefits from one primary instructional leader rather than three or four who observe less frequently. The more coaches involved, the less likely that the feedback—and thus growth—will be targeted and coordinated. This is the case for teachers, and it is also true for principals. Rather than have a literacy coach go to the school once a semester, a math coach a different

Weekly Schedule Template

Time	Monday	Tuesday	Wednesday	Thursday	Friday
6:00 AM					
:30					
7:00 AM					
:30					
8:00 AM					
:30					
9:00 AM					
:30					
10:00 AM					
:30					
11:00 AM					
:30					
12:00 PM					
:30					
1:00 PM					
:30					
2:00 PM					
:30					
3:00 PM					
:30					
4:00 PM					
:30					
5:00 PM					
:30					

month, and the principal manager just once a year, rethink the leadership model so that a particular person is the primary contact and coach for that school.

Let's look more closely at one example. You met Erin McMahon briefly in Chapter 3 on data-driven instruction. As instructional superintendent in Denver, she was responsible for managing fourteen schools. She had one deputy principal manager as her support. Here is how she organized her time:

- **Manage a subset of the schools directly—weekly or biweekly.** Erin took on seven of her fourteen schools directly and assigned seven to her deputy. For her seven schools, she visited them every other week for a two- to three-hour formal principal check-in, following the protocols in this book. Even though she was close to the 6:1 ratio that would have allowed to her visit every week, she limited herself to biweekly check-ins to allow her to still visit the other schools periodically (more on that in the next point).

- **Delegate the rest to the deputy—and join once a month.** For the other seven schools, the deputy visited them every week, and Erin would join him once a month. She didn't check in separately with the principal, because that might lead her and her deputy to give different messages on what to prioritize. Rather, she joined the deputy–principal check-ins so that she could observe the school and give both the deputy and that principal feedback that they could work on and practice during their check-ins.

Erin's example is just one way of doing this. For the principal managers reading this book who have large workloads, each context will be unique, and the staffing of the district will be different. There will be some cases where all your best efforts don't get you to 12:1. You will have to pick the schools you will prioritize, and work to push your larger organization to increase support for the rest. Again, a rethinking of district-wide coaching and instructional leadership can usually solve this problem. Often it's not a question of budget but of how we are spending our time. If this is not the case for you, that's where the next chapter comes in; it's about creating the right conditions for success for your district to make this possible.

Once you've gotten a focus on the six to twelve schools that you will work with weekly or biweekly, you can start to build your schedule.

Block Out External Commitments

Serena's first step is to flag any external commitments on her calendar that will keep her away from schools: district meetings, central office responsibilities, and so on. That's the one part of her schedule she can't adjust, so flagging it first gives her the ability to look with clear eyes at the parts she can.

Serena's Weekly Schedule: External Commitments

Time	Monday	Tuesday	Wednesday	Thursday	Friday
8:00 AM					
:30					
9:00 AM					District Meetings
:30					
10:00 AM					
:30					
11:00 AM	Superintendent Leadership Team Meeting				
:30					
12:00 PM					
:30					
1:00 PM					
:30					
2:00 PM					
:30					
3:00 PM					
:30					
4:00 PM					
:30					
5:00 PM					
:30					

What you will immediately notice is that with the exception of her superintendent leadership team meeting, all external meetings fall on Friday. This is intentional: it is a district-wide commitment to hold Monday through Thursday sacred for instructional leadership. This is a game-changing move: it allows you to lock in your work in schools. (In the next chapter—the Superintendent's Guide—we'll talk about the decisions that districts and organizations can make to provide this sort of sacred time for all their principal managers.)

Lock in Instructional Meetings and Other Activities

Next, Serena gives top priority to what makes the biggest difference for her students: her instructional meetings with her principals and their teams. These meetings are when Serena guides her leaders to perfect instruction and culture, giving them specific action steps and opportunities to practice—in short, they're when she does all the highest-leverage work described in this book. To do that work regularly, Serena makes sure to meet with each of her principals every week. (Serena has six schools; if you have twelve, you will shift to every other week, using the same time blocks shown here but over a two-week span.)

There are some key characteristics to Serena's schedule that should be highlighted:

- **Start with the exemplar—put him or her on Monday.** Serena sets her schedule such that she visits her top leader first, because that is the exemplar who will give her guidance on how to coach the rest. There is another advantage to scheduling the exemplar on Monday. Monday is the day that has the most holidays over the course of the school year. Losing your check-in for that week will be easiest with your highest-achieving principals.

- **Add a buffer after meetings with principals who need more support.** If you have a principal who is struggling, make sure to leave a buffer of extra time after the check-in. That will allow you to extend it for a longer time when you need to observe more, have additional practice, plan for difficult conversations, and so on.

- **Lock in leadership PD and team time.** Serena doesn't only lock in check-ins with her individual principals; she also locks in time with them as a team. Tuesday afternoons are reserved for monthly district-wide PD for instructional leadership. Each week this time is dedicated to a different group of instructional leaders: principals, coaches (e.g., assistant principals, instructional leaders) and principal managers. (Serena has her own PD block with her superintendent!) Think about the power of the Tuesday afternoon block: every instructional leader at every level has a

Serena's Weekly Schedule: External Commitments and Instructional Meetings

Time	Monday	Tuesday	Wednesday	Thursday	Friday
8:00 AM					
:30		Principal C Check-In (Struggling)			
9:00 AM	Principal A Check-In (Exemplar)		Principal E Check-In (Struggling)	Principal Team Meetings: Peer Walkthroughs and/or School Inspections (2/month)	District Meetings
:30					
10:00 AM					
:30					
11:00 AM	Superintendent Leadership Team Meeting	Principal D Check-In			
:30					
12:00 PM			Principal F Check-In		
:30					
1:00 PM					
:30	Principal B Check-In (2nd Exemplar)	District-Wide Instructional Leadership PD (Wk 1: principals) (Wk 2: APs) (Wk 3: principal managers)			
2:00 PM					
:30					
3:00 PM					
:30					
4:00 PM					
:30					
5:00 PM					
:30					

chance to participate in high-quality PD with his or her peers—and the impact on the school schedule is minimized by keeping it on Tuesdays.

The second team time for Serena is on Thursdays. That's when she can meet with her principals as a team, either to do follow-up practice from the Tuesday PD or to conduct a peer walkthrough and inspection of each other's schools. By designating Thursdays for these activities, Serena enables her principals to plan all their observations and check-ins to occur on the other days so that they never have to cancel to meet with Serena.

What has Serena done with this sort of schedule? She has prioritized instructional leadership, squeezing other commitments around what matters most. And she's done so while still leaving flexible time for other things that can, and will, arise.

A Word on . . . the Power of School Leadership Teams

Chapter 5 addressed extensively how to lead your principals as a team to create a "one school" culture and create peer support and accountability. There is another team you can impact as well: the instructional leadership team at each school.

The larger a school, the more important its instructional leadership team becomes in making sure the school runs effectively. To leverage your impact on the entire team and not just the principal, consider Erin McMahon's strategy: meet with them both.

Erin staggers her principal meetings so that the first meeting is with only the principal—that gives her dedicated personal time to develop the principal. In the subsequent meeting, she has the leadership team or key leader (e.g., the assistant principal) join the principal check-in. They do the same activities—walk around the school, practice their action steps, and so on—but they do them jointly.

In this way, the assistant principal isn't only getting coaching secondhand from the principal; she's getting developed directly by Erin. In one standing check-in, Erin is maximizing her impact.

Lock in Work Time for Big Projects

Finally, Serena locks in time for work on large projects. To protect that time, she makes sure these are two- to three-hour blocks of time during which she won't be interrupted. Serena can use this time for whatever work will make the biggest difference for her schools, from planning her check-ins and PD to sculpting a district-wide cultural system.

Serena's Weekly Schedule: External + Instructional + Work Time

Time	Monday	Tuesday	Wednesday	Thursday	Friday
8:00 AM					
:30		Principal C Check-In (Struggling)			
9:00 AM	Principal A Check-In (Exemplar)		Principal E Check-In (Struggling)		
:30					
10:00 AM				Principal Team Meetings: Peer Walkthroughs and/or School Inspections (2/month)	
:30					
11:00 AM	Superintendent Leadership Team Meeting	Principal D Check-In			District Meetings
:30					
12:00 PM					
:30					
1:00 PM	Principal B Check-In (2nd Exemplar)	District-Wide Instructional Leadership PD (Wk 1: principals) (Wk 2: APs) (Wk 3: principal managers)	Principal F Check-In		
:30					
2:00 PM					
:30					
3:00 PM	Big-Picture Work Time				Big-Picture Work Time
:30					
4:00 PM					
:30					
5:00 PM					
:30					

Congratulations! When you've completed all these steps, you've built the schedule of a master leader. Take a moment to reflect on everything this schedule accomplishes:

- A significant amount of your time is still free: you can devote that to any unforeseen challenges that arise.

- You're on the ground meeting with your principals and walking the halls of your schools for at least fifteen hours a week. That's time you can guarantee you'll spend working directly with leaders to support them in doing what matters most for learning.

- You've protected the time you need to maintain work time on ongoing projects. That way, you can be sure those projects will get done—while at the same time ensuring that they don't derail your most important instructional work.

Stop and Jot

Where might this schedule *not* work?

_____

_____

_____

_____

What changes could be made (personally or at the network level) to make this function more effectively?

_____

_____

_____

_____

How should your schedule align with that of other team members in your network?

_____

_____

_____

_____

DEFEND YOUR TIME

Once you've set up a schedule like this, how can you make sure it's feasible to maintain it? What follows are some best practices for sustainable time management that have been discovered by successful leaders across networks and districts.

- **Set sacred days district wide.** Maintaining time you've set aside to be in schools is extraordinarily difficult unless you set district-wide norms for all other meetings. At multiple districts I have supported that have made the change to instructional leadership, they have committed as a district to hold all non-school-based meetings on just one or two days a week (often Thursdays and Fridays), which sets Monday through Wednesdays as sacred times to be in the schools. Until you do this, no leader will be successful at maintaining a schedule that balances time in schools with time in his or her regional office. Locking in days for regional meetings, all-school walk-throughs, and so forth, and communicating that information to all members of your district team so that they know which days are sacred, are important cornerstones for making sure everyone can spend time on what matters most.

- **Reduce email traffic.** Scarcely anything can derail time for instructional leadership faster than email. You can save an immense amount of time by setting the expectation that principals will avoid emailing you unless it's a crisis that cannot wait until you check in with them.

- **Delegate administrative work.** Most of us have others working for us to whom we can delegate some of the administrative tasks of running schools. To protect your own time for instructional leadership, lean on the rest of your school management team to complete work that doesn't have to do with instruction, such as compliance and budgeting.

MANAGE YOUR TASKS

You've locked in your time to focus on instructional leadership, so one question remains: What will you do during each check-in? How will you stay on top of what every leader is doing week to week? This is where your task management comes into play.

Many of the tips here draw from a long line of time and task management experts who have had an influence on my work, from Michael Ambriz to Maia Heyck-Merlin, the author of *The Together Leader* (a great resource for managing your tasks as a school leader). These experts can go into much more detail about the art of task management, but I would recommend two great practices to make your schedule work. The next sections highlight how two effective principal managers put these into practice.

Set the Focus for Each Quarter

Although every principal has his or her own growth plan, it can be incredibly helpful for a principal manager to start with a general area of focus for each quarter of the year. Chi Tschang is a regional superintendent for Achievement First, and he uses the following areas of focus for each quarter. When I have shared these focus areas with other principal managers, they resonated deeply and gave managers clarity.

Setting a Quarterly Focus

Quarter 1—Student culture

- **Focus:** getting 100% of students to be engaged in learning
- **Key leadership levers:** student culture, observation and feedback
- **Key tool:** 30-Day Playbook
- **Quick reference:** Phases 1 and 2 for culture in the Get Better Faster Scope and Sequence

Quarter 2—Monitoring and weekly data meetings

- **Focus 1:** monitoring during class to see whether students are learning
- **Key leadership levers:** observation and feedback, data-driven instruction
- **Key tool:** peer walkthroughs
- **Quick reference:** Phase 2 for rigor in the Get Better Faster Scope and Sequence
- **Focus 2:** leading weekly data meetings to reteach more effectively
- **Key tool:** Weekly Data Meeting one-pager

Quarter 3: Discourse

- **Focus:** building teacher skill to lead effective discourse to deepen student thinking
- **Key leadership levers:** observation and feedback, planning
- **Key tool:** peer walkthroughs
- **Quick reference:** Phases 3 and 4 in the Get Better Faster Scope and Sequence

Quarter 4: Putting it all together

Think about the power of setting your focus like this. You can still differentiate for each principal—not holding back the principals who are ready to fly further and providing more support for struggling principals—but this can give you clarity on where to focus throughout the year.

Stop and Jot

What could you establish as your own areas for focus for each quarter of the year?

_____

_____

_____

_____

_____

Manage Your Tasks Each Week

When you set a common focus for all the schools you manage, you make it much easier to decide where to spend your time. Serena Savarirayan shows how. Here is her weekly schedule for the six schools she manages. She has set data-driven instruction as the core focus for this quarter. Look at how she lays out her tasks for each week.

Serena's Weekly Task List

School	10/23 Pacing Guide: Lesson Plans 6–9	10/30 Pacing Guide: Lesson Plans 10–14	11/6 Pacing Guide: Lesson Plans 15–18	11/13 Pacing Guide: Lesson Plans 19–22
All Schools	**DDI:** • Complete IA analysis meetings • Create leader action plans for 5–8 math and ELA	**Obs/Feedback:** • Conduct reteach lesson observations **DDI:** • Review student data from reteach lessons	**Obs/Feedback:** • Observe exemplar teachers to use to coach the others **DDI:** • Review student data from reteach lessons	**Obs/Feedback:** • Observe exemplar teachers to use to coach the others **DDI:** • Review student data from reteach lessons

School	10/23 Pacing Guide: Lesson Plans 6–9	10/30 Pacing Guide: Lesson Plans 10–14	11/6 Pacing Guide: Lesson Plans 15–18	11/13 Pacing Guide: Lesson Plans 19–22
	Planning: • Review school-based reteach lesson plans	• Lead WDM for power standard on IA 2	• Lead WDM for power standard on IA 2	• Lead WDM for power standard on IA 2
School A		8th math IA results meeting video and feedback	5th math WDM on standard (NS2)	5th ELA WDM 8th math WDM (systems of equations)
School B	Completed IA analysis with KF	**Culture:** Individual corrections and whole-class resets	**Culture:** Individual corrections and whole-class resets	6th math unit assessment with KF
School C		5th ELA WDM video review and feedback		8th ELA WDM 5th math WDM (dividing unit fractions)
School D			7th WDM: (inequalities) 7th ELA: IA results meeting video review 5th math co-observation (NF6)	8th math WDM: U2L18 (systems of equations) 7th math WDM video review
School E			8th Math co-observation, key lesson (systems of equations)	
School F		5th math IA results video review and feedback 7th math IA results video review and feedback 8th math IA results video review and feedback	8th ELA WDM (argumentation)	5th ELA WDM 6th math WDM (unit rate)

Here we can see the power of a focus for the quarter combined with differentiation for each principal. In one page, Serena can track her focus exactly. This makes planning for each meeting so much easier, and it allows her to keep singular attention on what matters most. The ripple effect on her management is significant—and it can be for you as well.

Stop and Jot

What could you do to improve your system for managing weekly tasks for each school you manage?

_____

_____

_____

_____

CONCLUSION

If this book offers a single message, it is that if you can master your time, you can master school leadership. Doing so requires focus, determination, and hard work. Yet as this chapter shows, it does not demand the impossible. On the contrary, the leaders in this book succeeded because they constantly worked to have the greatest impact in the *least* amount of time: the classroom walkthrough that fixes not only the teaching but also the leadership, the weekly data meeting that closes the gap on a standard as well as the principal's prompting, the PD session that creates entire networks of school leadership teams that are moving in the same direction. The result is clear: better schools that provide more for all students. Ultimately, then, the question is not whether it is feasible for principal managers to pursue these systems, but whether they can afford not to.

Core Idea

Ultimately, the question is not whether it is feasible for principal managers to pursue these systems but whether they can afford not to.

Stop Here

(STOP) The next chapter is specifically designated for superintendents or, more broadly speaking, the leaders who make district-wide decisions that affect the work of the principal manager—decisions like which interim assessments your district will use, the curriculum, when district meetings are held, and principal manager staffing. If you do *not* have these responsibilities and are primarily a principal manager, you can skip Chapter 7. You have everything you need to drive change in your leadership, and Part 4 is available to you if you want professional development materials to use with fellow principal managers.

If you are a superintendent, have district-wide decision-making power, are both the principal manager and the superintendent, or are part of an organization that works with districts in support of their principals, read on! The next chapter will address the nuts and bolts of setting up your district or organization to succeed.

Pulling the Lever: Action Planning Worksheet

Finding the Time

Planning for Action

- What tools from this chapter will you use to lead your schools?

_____

_____

_____

- What are your next steps to strengthen your time and task management?

_____

_____

_____

Action	Date

Chapter 7

A Superintendent's Guide to Creating the Conditions for Success

Ogden, Utah. Caddo Parish, Louisiana. Gallup, New Mexico. Cincinnati, Ohio. Clark County, Nevada. These cities are all over the United States. What brings them together is that in all of them, leaders are committed to improving student achievement across their schools, and their work has made an impact at scale.

The layers of leadership it takes to drive results like these vary depending on the size of the district. If you work in a small district, the principal manager and superintendent are one and the same! For a larger district, serving as superintendent entails managing a team of principal managers to make your schools excellent.

The work of this sort of superintendent merits a book in and of itself. For the purposes of this chapter, however, we'll consider one the most important parts of that work: creating the conditions for success so that your principals and principal managers can fly.

Essentially, this means meeting three key conditions:

1. **Maximizing time in schools for principals and managers.** Maximize the time principals and principal managers spend in schools by creating the proper schedules for managers and leaders and removing obstacles from their path.

2. **Building data-driven instruction systems.** Build the right foundation to drive student learning: intentional, high-quality assessments; data-driven curriculum; data meeting structures; and PD.

3. **Providing flexibility for turnaround support.** Implement basic systems for your schools in turnaround to support the overall district vision: flexible teacher and leader hiring and intentional monthly maps or ninety-day plans.

Prioritizing these actions means prioritizing instructional quality as the core of the superintendent's role. In too many districts, this is far from certain. Just as principals often find themselves fighting fires, superintendents often find themselves bogged down by a daily parade of noninstructional tasks. Although the shift in outlook described here is significant, it offers an unparalleled chance to drive student success. Let's see how to make this happen.

Core Idea

To create the right district-wide conditions for success, implement the following three conditions:

1. **Maximizing time in schools:** maximize the time principals and principal managers spend in schools

2. **Data-driven instruction systems:** build the right foundation for effective data-driven instruction

3. **Flexible support for turnaround:** implement basic systems for your schools in turnaround

---

MAXIMIZE TIME IN SCHOOLS

To raise achievement, school leaders need to spend time on instructional and cultural leadership. This means that superintendents need to create the culture that maximizes principals' and managers' time in schools—something easier said than done when there are so many noninstructional factors that can cause them to do just the opposite. Here are some simple steps to maximize time in schools.

Get Principal Managers into Each School Biweekly

If principal managers are to be instructional leaders devoted to developing—not just evaluating—school leaders, they need time to coach those leaders in their schools. The starting point is consistent visits: a minimum of biweekly coaching sessions. As Chapter 6 (Finding the Time) showed, successful managers find that those sessions must run at least ninety minutes—and more often two to three hours—to provide sufficient time to monitor the school and coach the principal. For this to work requires a manager–principal ratio of 6:1 for weekly visits or 12:1 for biweekly visits.

If your district already has a 12:1 ratio, move on to the next section! But how do you achieve that ratio if you have principal managers in charge of twenty-five schools apiece? By delegating and distributing your schools among everyone assigned to support them. Often in districts where principal managers have twenty-five schools, there are also deputy principal managers and full-time district coaches supporting those schools. Shifting from having multiple people all providing sporadic support to a single school to having one central person supporting each school will get most districts to a ratio of 12:1 or less, which enables real coaching to happen.

In cases where even that is not possible and you don't have the financial means to change the situation, you are better served deeply coaching a subset of the schools than visiting all schools superficially. Not working with all schools is highly unfortunate, but if this is what you must do, make sure your managers keep some of the exemplar schools in addition to struggling ones. If they don't see the exemplar, they don't have the tools to help the struggling school.

Stop and Jot

Principal Managers in Schools

What is the current ratio of principal managers to schools in your district or organization? If it is high, how could you distribute schools more effectively among your central office support to maximize the coaching each principal receives?

_____

_____

_____

_____

_____

Getting a good ratio of principal managers to schools is the first step to maximizing time in schools. The other parts involve reducing the time spent on everything else.

Create Sacred Days for School-Based Leadership

When I ask school leaders about the biggest obstacles to implementing the Leverage Leadership model, one of the most common responses is the number of meetings that pull them out of schools to central office meetings that have little to do with instruction. The worst aspect of this challenge is that these meetings vary in timing, so leaders struggle to make a consistent schedule that they can follow.

The best advice for solving this? Create "sacred days" during which no meetings can occur for principal managers or principals. We saw in Chapter 6 that Serena Savarirayan's network has all organization meetings on Fridays. This can easily become your district-wide policy: all meetings involving school-based staff (including principal managers) may only occur on one day of the week.

Think about the impact of that simple decision. A principal and a manager can lock in consistent schedules Monday through Thursday that allow them to focus on all aspects of leadership. They can keep Fridays open, and when there is no district meeting, they gain additional time in their schools. When there is such a meeting, they don't have to reschedule anything and can keep up their overall leadership.

Look at Serena's schedule in Chapter 6 to see what such a calendar could look like.

Change Email Culture

After noninstructional meetings, the second biggest time drain that can send school leaders from classrooms to their desks is email management. In addition to the time it takes to respond to all the emails, dealing with email sends you to your phone or computer, where even more distractions can keep you from instructional leadership. Recognizing this, Erin McMahon made a commitment to dramatically reduce the time she—and everyone else in her school district—spent on email by setting these simple norms:

- All emails from the central office need to come from a single person who consolidates all information.

- If the item can wait until an upcoming check-in or meeting, don't send it via email. (This sounds simple, and it is; it is one of the easiest ways to reduce time spent dealing with email!)

Provide Public Support

One of the key roles that a superintendent can play to make learning fly is to "block and tackle": remove obstacles from principals' and managers' work so that they can focus completely on teaching and learning. In addition to reducing the amount of time leaders are out of school, Hannah Lofthus makes sure to publicly support the actions her leaders take in their schools to make them great—especially if the action in question is a change that might face resistance. That gives her leaders "cover," and sends the message to their staff that what they're being asked to do is important.

Remove or Reduce "Administrivia"

Education has an incredible number of layers of compliance and administrative tasks that can sink many a well-intentioned principal and principal manager. Compliance has a role, but effective superintendents like Hannah and Erin are careful never to let it get in the way of instructional leadership. One of the most important actions they take is to reduce the amount of noninstructional work that makes its way to the principals' and managers' desks:

- Push 95 percent of compliance and administrative work to people other than principals and principal managers: select a compliance leader from the rest of the school staff.

- Cut any worksheet or task that isn't actually needed. (You'd be surprised by how many of those exist within your schools!)

BUILD DATA-DRIVEN INSTRUCTION SYSTEMS

As discussed extensively in Chapter 3, your district needs to be able to answer two fundamental questions: How do you know if students are learning? When they are not, what do you do about it? Principals and principal managers will do the lion's share of the work on these questions. The most important work Erin faces in supporting them is to make sure that the key systems mentioned in Chapter 3 are locked into place:

- **Quality assessments.** Remember that less is more. One set of quality interim assessments is ideal to be able to drive instruction—not just measure it.

- **Foundational curriculum and lesson plans.** A rigorous, quality curriculum and lower-caliber instruction can do more for your schools than high-quality instruction paired with poor curriculum!

- **Data meeting structures.** All the curriculum and assessments in the world won't matter if teachers aren't changing their tactics in response to student learning. Regular teacher team data meetings lock that into place and are one of the biggest predictors of student achievement.

- **Professional development.** Erin makes sure that all staff members have received PD on the power of data-driven instruction; it helps them focus on the learning and not just the teaching.

PROVIDE FLEXIBLE SUPPORT FOR TURNAROUNDS

Once you reach a certain size as a district or organization, you are pretty much guaranteed to have a few schools that are struggling more than the others. Many of those get to a place where the leader needs to start over to turn the school around. When a school reaches this stage, leaders must take additional actions beyond everything else we've described so far:

- **Provide more time.** For turnaround schools, the principal manager needs more time to support the principal. "In districts that have gotten multiple turnaround schools to improve, spending three to four hours per week providing side-by-side support in that school has been one of the top predictors of success," comments William Robinson, executive director of the University of Virginia Partnership for Leaders in Education. Make sure that the principal manager supporting that school locks in longer time blocks to support the principal in everything he or she will be doing to improve the school.

- **Make room for flexible teacher hiring.** When a school has struggled tremendously, a leader needs to have the flexibility to hire the staff who are invested in turning around the school. In nearly every successful turnaround that I have studied, the leader had the autonomy to select part or all of his or her staff. Thus the leader is working with teachers who have the will to make the turnaround—then the leader can build the skill.

- **Keep the focus on the super-levers.** Data-driven instruction and student culture are called super-levers for a reason: they are the foundational levers that drive a school to succeed. Turnaround schools need to keep the focus on these two levers—and nothing else. Other levers can wait until the later years of the turnaround.

- **Create monthly maps and/or ninety-day plans.** With so much going on in turnaround, time and task management tools are a must. Turnaround schools particularly benefit from tools like ninety-day plans, breaking down the year into chunks to focus on key actions and then change course based on the results.

CONCLUSION

When we look at the results of leaders like Serena and Erin, it might appear as if they have a magic touch that makes multiple schools astoundingly successful by sheer association. But the reality is that each of the steps they take to replicate success district wide are concrete—and replicable. They don't have to be everywhere at once; they simply need to set the conditions so that they, and the leaders they manage, can always be in the right place at the right time to drive student learning.

Pulling the Lever: Action Planning Worksheet
A Superintendent's Guide

Planning for Action

- What tools from this chapter will you use to lead your schools? Check all that you will use.

  ☐ Maximizing time in schools

  ☐ Data-driven instruction systems

  ☐ Flexible support for turnarounds

  ☐ Other: _____

- How will you modify these guidelines to meet your district's needs?

  _____

  _____

  _____

• What are your next steps for setting the conditions for success as a superintendent?

Action	Date

Conclusion

Erin McMahon, whom you first met in the Chapter 3 of this book, has this final piece of advice for principal managers: it's behind-the-scenes work. Principals will be recognized more readily than you will for the work of leading schools—and that's just as it should be. "We have this mistaken notion in education that the higher up you go, the more important you are," Erin says. "But the opposite is true. We are here to serve the principals, who are here to serve the teachers, who are here to serve the students."

Ultimately, the power of the actions in this book is that they enable you to serve more students more effectively.

You read this book because you are committed to changing the lives of as many students as you can. The systems outlined here will get you there. Jeanine, LaKimbre, Juliana, Hannah, Jesse, Erin, Tera, Kelly, and Serena all succeeded because of their systems, but also because they held this as their core commitment. Commitment to students, combined with the right actions, is the driving force of change. Take both of these into your work, and your service will make a difference.

Part 4

Professional Development

Chapter 8

Workshops: Overview and Highlights

Use these professional development workshops to train other leaders to implement the seven key levers of leadership featured in this book.

Workshops for Principal Managers Included in This Book

- Data-Driven Instruction for Principal Managers (Chapter 3)

- Leading Student Culture for Principal Managers (Chapter 4)

What workshop materials will you find in the text?

- A cover page that highlights the workshop's goals and intended audience

- A *small segment* of the full-length presenter's notes to be used while presenting the workshop

What additional workshop materials will you find on the DVD?

- The full-length presenter's notes to be used while presenting the workshop, which include a list of all materials, copies, and videos to be used in the session

- The PowerPoint presentation that accompanies each workshop

- The handouts you'll need to provide for each workshop

- The core videos that will be used in the session

Workshops for principals—look in our other books

- In *Driven by Data*:
  - o Data-Driven Instruction 101

- In *Leverage Leadership 2.0*:
  - o Observation and Feedback 101 (Chapter 3)
  - o Leading Professional Development (Chapter 4)
  - o Student Culture (Chapter 5)

- In *Get Better Faster*:
  - o Data-Driven Instruction 201: Weekly Data Meetings
  - o Observation and Feedback 201: Real-time Feedback

DATA-DRIVEN INSTRUCTION FOR PRINCIPAL MANAGERS

What's the Goal?

Make principal managers excellent at leading principals in data-driven instruction. By the end of the workshop, principal managers will know how to

- Identify key patterns across multischool data and identify the right action steps.

- Lead effective meetings with principals to quicken their development in leading data-driven instruction.

Who's the Audience?

Anyone who leads principals, either formally or informally.

This may include superintendents, assistant superintendents, school chiefs, executive directors—this list is endless! The "circle of leadership" extends also to school boards, state departments of education, principal training organizations, school turnaround programs, and any organization devoted to developing school leaders. If your role is to make principals better, then this workshop applies to you!

When to Use It

Best Time

Right before the school year begins, or right after a round of interim assessments. This gives participants the most direct opportunity to put what they learn into action.

Other Times That Work

Any other point during the school year.

Data-Driven Instruction for Principal Managers—Session Plan

Timing: 8:00 a.m.–5:00 p.m.
1 hour for lunch, two 15-minute breaks

Objectives
1. Identify key patterns across multischool data and identify the right action steps.
2. Lead effective meetings with principals to quicken their development in leading data-driven instruction.
Document(s)
See Separate Guide

See It–Name It–Do It Legend

S = See It: airtight activities that leads participants to the right conclusion mostly on their own

N = Name It: lead participants to name the keys to the action, then add formal language at the end

D = Do It: put the principles into practice

R = Reflect: participants quietly analyze, then generate conclusions or takeaways

Agenda: *How will you display the agenda during the session?*	
Mins	***Description of Instruction (Living the Learning Type in Parenthesis)***
INTRODUCTION	

10	**Introduction (N)**
	• Table introductions (Slides 1–2).
	   o Share your role, how many schools you manage, and the biggest challenge in your role.
	• Poll the room.
	   o How many manage 1–5 schools?
	   o 6–10 schools?
	   o 11–15 schools?
	   o 16–25?
	   o 25+?
	   o *NOTE: we all have different loads, and we will try to serve everyone!*
	• Share personal intro (Slide 3).
	   o Deliver a personal introduction that briefly tells your participants why you're prepared to lead them and why this work is important to you.
	• Introduce the course.
	   o The question is not how can we find principal stars, but how can we create them?

5	**Norms and Goals (N)** • Share the norms (Slide 4): o "Can we all agree to these norms?"

5	**Findings from the Field (N)**
	• Interviews from strongest school leaders (Slide 5–6).
	   o Exceptional school leaders are not miracle workers; they are just relentless about how they spend their time.
	   o And they lead others to do the same.
	• Introduce the Levers of Leadership (Slides 7–10).
	• Share the goals for this workshop (Slide 11).

10	**Hook (S-N)**
	• Context (Slides 12–13, 1 min).
	   o Find an engaging clip of an orchestra conductor modeling and giving feedback to their musicians.
	• Share key questions (Handout Page 1).
	   o "What does ___ do to help his or her student improve?"
	   o "What makes her coaching so effective?"
	• Show ___ (video clip you have selected).
	• Partner-share (1 min).
	• Core Ideas (Slide 14).
	   o As the conductor, you no longer play the music, but there is no symphony without you.
	
	Agenda (Slide 15)
	• We will practice looking @ global data and determining the highest-leverage focus areas.
	• We will build the systems to implement principal management.
	• We will practice coaching our leaders by leveraging our data to drive student achievement.

MONITORING THE SCHOOL	

10	**Using Data Case Study—Round 1 (Experience the Non-Exemplar) (S)**
	• Context (Slides 16–17, 2 min).
	   o Challenge with DDI as a PM: responsible for many schools
	   o One of the most critical decisions is where to focus.

	o We'll start with IA data: Dashboard of data from IA 1 for all schools you manage. o You must decide where to focus; you cannot dive deeply into everything. • Task—Chart (Slide 18, 8 min). o Review the data. o What are your top five actions as a result of this data? o What would be the focus of your one-on-one check-ins with principals next week? o What would you do at a principal team meeting?
5	**Spar (N)** • Share your action steps with your partner (Slide 19). o Discuss: What are the strengths and limitations of your action steps? • Spar with Paul Bambrick-Santoyo's Action Steps (Slide 20). o Reveal "Paul's Action Steps" • Share out. o What are your key takeaways? • Core Idea (Slide 21). o Start from the exemplar. o You cannot fix the error until you know what you are looking for.
25	**Using Data Case Study—Round 2—Exemplar Data (S)** • Context (Slide 22). o Round 2—you have been given this additional data (3 min): [in tab 5]. o Simple network summary (simple version of) Chiger analysis (standard analysis, outlier teachers, reteach lesson). o Student work samples from seventh-grade ELA for IA 1 from School H and School D, o Weekly Data Meeting action planning tracker (of school D and school H seventh-grade teams), • Task (Slide 23, 15 min). o Review the additional data.

	o What are your top five actions as a result of this data?
	o What would be the focus of your one-on-one check-ins with principals next week? What would you do at a principal team meeting?
	• Chart.
10	**Spar (N)**

Spar (N)

- Share your action steps with your partner.

  o Discuss: What are the strengths and limitations of your action steps?

- Spar with Paul Bambrick-Santoyo's action steps (Slide 24).

  o Reveal "Paul's Top Action Steps."

Paul's Top Actions (N)

1. Develop key guidelines for identifying the claim in informational texts.

    - How to annotate

    - How to write subclaims

    - How to notice shifts in claims

    - How to synthesize a final claim

2. Work leader/teacher from School D to lead a cross-campus PD on reading for claim and providing the appropriate evidence using their skills from step 1.

3. Create a simple checklist to monitor the following on school walk-throughs with leaders:

    - Monitor the percentage of students on task during independent practice.

      o Pen-to-paper: they are answering questions.
      o Annotations: they are annotating texts/tasks/questions before answering them.
      o Answers: they have the right answers.

4. Add Exemplar student responses from School D teacher to the weekly data meetings at other schools.

    - Pair-share and share out (Slide 25, 5 min).

      o What are the biggest differences between our first round of action steps and our second?
      o What are your big takeaways for analyzing data at your schools?

	• Core Idea (Slide 26).
	   o You can't correct what you don't detect.
	   o Have the right data in hand to monitor not only the result, but also *how* we got there.

10	**Keys to Using Data Effectively as a Principal Manager (N)** • Share findings (Slides 27–29).

10	**Reflection (R)**
	• Q&A.
	   o Ask facilitator questions about how to collect the data.
	• Individual (Slide 30).
	   o What are the current gaps between these guiding principles and my own management?
	   o What systems do I need to build/improve have to make this happen?
	• Pair-Share.

10	**Build Your Systems—Results Meeting Protocol (D)**
	• Context (Slide 31).
	   o "Now it's your turn to plan how you can build data systems for your schools."
	   o "We're going to use a Results Meeting protocol to plan effectively and efficiently."
	• Topics (Slide 32).
	   o **School data dashboard:** building the dashboard to help you run your schools
	   o **Preparing for principal check-ins:** creating systems to for principals to be ready with all necessary data for check-ins
	• **Network analysis**: identifying the individuals and training them to do network analysis to identify patterns/trends for your focus
	• Instructions (Slides 33–35, Tab 6).
	   o Walkthrough protocol (see one-pager and PPT)
	   o Emphasize: *you must chart.*

30	**Build Your Systems—Results Meeting (D)**
	• Identify roles: timer, facilitator, recorder (2 min).
	• Brainstorm proposed solutions (10 min).
	• Reflection: feasibility of each idea (5 min).
	• Consensus and put in calendar: When will the tasks happen? Who will complete them? (10 min)
2	**Reflection (R)**
	• Reflection (Slide 36).
	o What are your key takeaways for using data to drive principals?

Break (15 min)

MONITORING THE PRINCIPAL

5	**Introduction to Principal Support**
	• Context (Slide 37).
	o Your data is in hand.
	o Now it is time to see how the principal is leading to support a change in that data.
5	**Introduction to Principal Action Steps (S-N)**
	• Context (Slide 38).
	o We don't spend a lot of time talking about the right action step for a principal; that is a big reason why we often lack clarity in coaching them!
	• Skim the Leverage Leadership Sequence of Action Steps for Principals (Slide 39, Tab 2, 2 min).
	o What are the key characteristics of the action steps for principals across each lever?
	• Core Idea (Slide 40).
	o You cannot fix the execution without the right plan in place.
	o Plan. Roll out. Execute. Monitor.
	• Read DDI section of the Leverage Leadership Sequence of Action Steps for Principals (Slide 41, 2 min).
	o Put a star (★) next to all the gaps for the principals you currently lead.
	o Put a double star (★★) beside the action steps that are highest leverage to start with right away.

35	**Principal Case Study 1, Part 1—Student Work Analysis (D):** *NOTE: Film a weekly data meeting of one of your principals and collect the corresponding student work to use for this case study.*
	• Instructions (Slides 42–43).
	o Read the standard, then review the teacher exemplar and student work.
	o Identify the conceptual misunderstanding that is keeping students from mastering this action step.
	• Individual work (15 min).
	• Small-group work—chart (Slide 44, 10 min).
	• Gallery walk (2 min).
	o Which are the strongest action steps?
	• Spar with facilitator's action steps (Slide 45).
	o Reveal "student action steps."
	o *NOTE: Write your own action steps based on the case study you have selected.*
25	**Principal Case Study 1, Part 2: Video Analysis—Identifying the Right Action Step (D)** • Turn and Talk—Activate Knowledge.
	o Recall your PD on weekly data meetings: what are the key pieces to an effective weekly data meeting?
	o *NOTE: If principal managers have not taken the PD on data-driven instruction for principals, add an opportunity to learn about weekly data meetings and introduce the Weekly Data Meeting one-pager.*
	• Context.
	o "Now that we know what we need to have in place in order to lead meetings focused on the right things—deep and quality data, we are going to work on getting better at leading the actual meetings."
	o "We are about to practice coaching a principal on Leading Weekly Data Meetings."
	o "In this video, the teacher teaches a remedial high school math course. We are going to watch a clip of the data meeting."
	o The data the principal has is in Tab 6 (review before watching video).

	• **Watch Case Study Video Clip (selected by you)** (Slide 46).
	• Individual Reflection—Use Leverage Leadership Sequence of Action Steps for Principals.
	o What is the key action step for the leader in this meeting?
	o What additional data do you need to coach her even better?
10	**Video Case Study 1—Chart It (D)**
	• Chart in small groups.
	o What is the key action step for the leader in this meeting?
	o What additional data do you need to coach her even better?
5	**Spar with Each Other and the Exemplar (D)**
	• Peer review: (5 min).
	o What do you like about others' action steps? Which is strongest?
	o What additional forms of data would you want your principal to incorporate?
10	**Facilitator's Action Step for the Leader (R)**
	NOTE: Change these action steps for your own case study.
	• Reveal facilitator's action step (Slide 47).
	• Create a teacher/student exemplar.
	o Articulate how the exemplar exemplifies the standard.
	o Articulate what a student would say to justify their answer.
	• Sample for this task.
	o Absolute value is the distance of the answer from the origin.
	o To solve $|x - b| < c$, you must create two inequalities to replace the absolute value: $x - b < c$ and $x - b > -c$.
	o In this way the distance from the original is equal on both sides of the inequality.
	• Large-group share out (if time).
5	**Reflection (R)**
	• Core Idea (Slide 48).
	o If you don't know the data, you cannot monitor for results.
	• What are your takeaways for giving feedback to your school leaders?

LEADING STUDENT CULTURE FOR PRINCIPAL MANAGERS

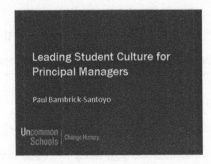

What's the Goal?

Make principal managers excellent at leading principals in student culture. By the end of the workshop, principal managers will know how to

- Identify highest-leverage action steps for leaders in rolling out school routines, practicing school routines, and leading school routines.

- Develop principals effectively in leading student culture.

Who's the Audience?

Anyone who leads principals, either formally or informally.

This may include superintendents, assistant superintendents, school chiefs, executive directors—this list is endless! The "circle of leadership" extends also to school boards, state departments of education, principal training organizations, school turnaround programs, and any organization devoted to developing school leaders. If your role is to make principals better, then this workshop applies to you!

When to Use It

Best Time

Right before the school year begins.

This gives participants the most direct opportunity to impact student culture for the long run.

Other Times That Work

In the spring, leading into planning for the next school year.

Leading Student Culture for Principal Managers

Timing: 8 a.m.–4 p.m.
45-minute lunch, two 15-minute breaks

Objectives
1. Identify highest-leverage action steps for leaders in rolling out school routines, practicing school routines, and leading school routines.
2. Develop principals effectively in leading student culture.

Document(s)
See Separate Guide

See It–Name It–Do It Legend

S = See It: airtight activities that leads participants to the right conclusion mostly on their own

N = Name It: lead participants to name the keys to the action, then add formal language at the end

D = Do It: put the principles into practice

R = Reflect: participants quietly analyze, then generate conclusions or takeaways

---

Agenda: *How will you display the agenda during the session?*	
Mins	***Description of Instruction (Living the Learning Type in Parenthesis)***
START WITH THE "NAME IT"	

5	**A Guide for Name it—Principal Action Steps by Lever (S, N)**
	• Independent task: read thru the Student Culture section (Slide 13).
	   ○ Put a star (★) next to the action steps that will be highest leverage for the principals you currently lead.
	   ○ Put a double star (★★) beside the action steps you'd like to use right away.
	   ○ (If time) Review other levers.

- Pair-Share.
  - o What actions of Student Culture from the scope and sequence will be most important for my principals this year?
- (If time) Large-group share out.
- Summarize areas of focus for the group.

Monitoring the School/Principal	

10	**Case Study 1: Choosing the Best Action Step (D)**
	• Intro (Slides 14–15).
	  o Let's apply!
	  o Norm: these leaders are our *heroes*.
	• Context.
	  o NOTE: *Give the needed context for the clip that you show.*
	• **Watch video case study of your own school leader.**
	• ID the top action step you would give.

10	**Chart your Action Steps (D)**
	• Individual (Slide 16, 2 min).
	  o Write your gap and action step.
	• Chart in small groups—Use your Leverage Leadership Sequence of Actions Steps for Principals and Get Better Faster Scope and Sequence as your guide (7 min).
	  o What's the root cause of the problem?
	  o What's the most precise action step?

15	**"Spar" with Each Other and the Exemplar (D)**
	• Peer review: (5 min).
	  o What do you like about others' action steps? Which is strongest?
	• Large-group share out.
	• **Reveal facilitator's top action step** (Slides 17–18).
	NOTE: *These are just samples. Rewrite to match your own video case study. Use the Leverage Leadership Sequence of Action Steps for Principals as a guide.*
	  o For the leader: Become the model of presence in whole school moments.
	    o Square up and stand still when giving a direction (verbal or nonverbal).

  o Do not talk over when giving a direction—ensure all students are tracking and silent before you speak.

  o Do it again when routines are not crisp.

 o For the school: Define/redefine the school-wide vision for lunch transition and include all student actions and teacher actions.

  o Script the routine so that all transitions are clear (e.g., when to stop eating, when to stop talking, when to pass trash, when to stand and leave, etc.) and all roles are clear (students, teachers, leaders).

  o Model the routine as the teacher with teachers playing the role of students.

  o Model the appropriate leader/teacher response to student error in the routine.

  o Have teachers practice the routine and pause to give real-time feedback (RTF).

  o Be present during all lunch transitions and give RTF and precise praise to students and teachers.

- Large-group share out.
- Core Idea (Slide 19).

10	**Case Study 2: Choosing the Best Action Step (D)**

- Intro (Slide 20).

 o Let's try again.

- Context.

 o *NOTE: Give the needed context for the clip that you show.*

- Key question (Slide 20).

 o ID the top action step you would give.

- **Watch video case study of your own school leader.**

10	**Action Steps Lightning Practice—Whiteboard (D)**

- Individual (5 min).

 o Write action step on whiteboard.

- Spar (5 min).

 o Reveal action steps to each other, and share Paul's action step.

	• **Reveal facilitator's top action step** (Slide 21).
	NOTE: These are just samples. Rewrite to match your own video case study. Use the Leverage Leadership Sequence of Action Steps for Principals as a guide.
	
	  o For the leader: When rolling out a school system.
	
	    o Model the entire routine prior to breaking down each part so that teachers can see the whole vision.
	
	    o Increase ratio and engagement by integrating reflection questions such as "Why will this routine help us change classes efficiently?" "What is the impact of a common phrase to end and start every class?"
	
	    o Pause and use changes of cadence to emphasize the most important phrases.

10	**Core Idea and Reflection (R)**
	• Core Idea (Slide 22).
	
	  o We follow what you *do*, not what you say.
	
	  o Improve the leader *actions* to improve the teachers—and the students.
	
	• Reflection (Slide 23).
	
	  o What are your big takeaways for how to write quality action steps?
	
	• Large-group share out.

MONITORING AND COACHING THE PRINCIPAL: SEE IT. NAME IT.	

1	**Introduction**
	• Context (Slides 24).
	
	  o Now that we have practiced naming the action step for the school and the principal, let's focus on coaching the principal to implement those action steps. What does it look like when instead of working on DDI you are working on student culture? What follows is a set of exemplar clips which will allow us to see principal managers in action.
	
	  o You will remember from yesterday—framework for effective meetings: reveal check-in template (if haven't already).
	
	  o We'll begin with the "See It."

10	**See It: See the Exemplar and the Gap**
	• Context (Slides 25–26).
	  o Hannah Lofthus is a principal manager in Kansas City, Missouri.
	  o Principal is working to improve her secondary leader on how to deal with students sent out of class.
	  o Principal has a strong vision for student culture.
	  o Working to get students sent out of class back to class as quickly as possible.
	  o Example in this video: student took lotion from a peer and refused to give it back.
	• Key question.
	  o What actions does Hannah take to support her principal in coaching her?
	• **Watch PM of LL 2.0 Clip 14.**
	• Pair-Share.
	• Share out.
	• Name It (Slides 27–28).
	  o See the exemplar.
	    o *Unpack the exemplar:* what would happen in a perfect world?
	    o "What is the thinking we want her doing?"
	    o "Why is that the highest leverage action?"
	  o See the gap.
	  o Name It.
	    o Create an action step for the *teacher* as well as the leader when that is needed to fix the problem.

10	**See It: See the Exemplar and Name the Gap (S, N)**
	• Context (Slide 29).
	  o Here Hannah is debriefing the school culture rehearsal that she just observed her principal leading.
	  o They were watching the school's grade level leaders leading their teams in rehearsing the end of breakfast and transition to the classroom.

<table>
<tr>
<td></td>
<td>

- o A couple of those grade level leaders struggled to model the routine effectively.
- o Hannah and her principal are now in their office debriefing.
- Key question.
- o What actions does Hannah take to push her principal's development in leading student culture?
- **Watch PM of LL 2.0 Clip 11.**
- Pair-Share.
- Share out.
- Name It (Slide 30).
  - o See the model . . .
    - o Hannah models what she should have seen.
  - o . . . and See the Gap . . . .
    - o "She corrected it but let them keep going. Why is that ineffective?"
  - o Name It—for the coach.
    - o "What is a transferable coaching structure you want her to use?"
  - o Name It—for the leader.
    - o "Before you leave the room, what should you do?"
    - o "So your leader action step is . . ."

</td>
</tr>
<tr>
<td>5</td>
<td>

Reflection (R)
- Reflect (Slide 31).
  - o What are your takeaways for developing leaders?
  - o What key moves will you adopt for the See It and Name It portion of your leading student culture meetings?

</td>
</tr>
</table>

Notes

Introduction

1. Alison Eldridge, "John Williams: American Composer and Conductor," *Encyclopaedia Britannica*, March 3, 2018, available at https://www.britannica.com/biography/John-Williams-American-composer-and-conductor.

2. "John Williams Biography," The Biography.com website, March 15, 2018, available at https://www.biography.com/people/john-williams-9532526.

3. Leithwood, Louis, and Anderson have ranked leadership as "second only to classroom instruction" as a determining factor as to what students learn in school; Branch, Hanushek, and Rivkin have found that effective principals improve student achievement by multiple months per year, whereas less effective principals lower achievement by the same amount. Leithwood, Louis, and Anderson and Branch, Hanushek and Rivkin are cited in Ben Klompus, *Scaling Instructional Improvement: Designing a Strategy to Develop the Leaders of Leaders* (doctoral dissertation, 2016; downloadable from https://dash.harvard.edu/handle/1/27013352). Further, Hattie has shown that "instructional leadership"—consistently believing that teacher actions shape student outcomes and delivering feedback to teachers, among other things—has a far higher impact on student learning than "transformational leadership," in which leaders focus on inspiring staff, setting common goals, and giving teachers autonomy. John Hattie, "High-Impact Leadership," *Educational Leadership* 72, no. 5 (February 2015): 36–40.

4. Jon Saphier and Pia Durkin write extensively on instructional leadership by principal managers as a cornerstone of school development at scale in "Supervising Principals: How Central Office Administrators Can Improve Teaching and

Learning in the Classroom: The Missing Link for Scaling Up School Improvement," September 21, 2011, available through the Research for Better Teaching website at http://rbteach.com/sites/default/files/supervising_and_coaching_principals_ saphier.pdf. Success in districts where principal managers have refocused their attention on instructional leadership has also been documented by Amy Saltzman in "Revising the Role of Principal Supervisor," *Phi Delta Kappan* 98, no. 2 (October 2016): 52–57. John T. Fitzsimons shares his personal journey from distant administrator to on-the-ground principal coach in "The Struggle to Supervise Principals," *School Administrator* 73, no. 6 (June 2016): 12.

Chapter 1

1. From the Teaching Trust 2017 Impact Report, available at https://static1 .squarespace.com/static/57ff97e8e4fcb510d48ca31b/t/5a9ea8c871c10b81e4343b86/ 1520347342165/Teaching+Trust+2017+Impact+Report.pdf.

Chapter 2

1. Daniel Coyle, *The Talent Code* (Random House, 2009), 82–84.

Chapter 3

1. Dan DeWitt, "Former Brooksville Resident LaKimbre Brown Is an Education Superstar," *Tampa Bay Times,* June 19, 2014, http://www.tampabay.com/news/education/ k12/former-brooksville-resident-lakimbre-brown-is-an-education-superstar/2185141.

2. Liana Heitin Loewus, "Study: Give Weak Teachers Good Lesson Plans, Not Professional Development," *Education Week,* July 12, 2016, http://blogs.edweek.org/ edweek/curriculum/2016/07/study_give_teachers_lesson_plans_not_professional_ development.html?cmp=SOC-SHR-FB.

3. Rick Hess, http://blogs.edweek.org/edweek/rick_hess_straight_up/2015/05/superin tendents_perspective_on_teacher_leadership.html.

Chapter 4

1. Kyle Palmer, "This Kansas City Charter School Has Been Tapped as the Best in Missouri," KCUR 89.3, November 13, 2015, available at http://kcur.org/post/ kansas-city-charter-school-has-been-tapped-best-missouri#stream/0.

2. "Academic Results," Ewing Marion Kauffman School website, available at http://www.kauffmanschool.org/en/Results/Academic-Results.aspx.

Chapter 5

1. "Leadership Prep Ocean Hill Charter School—Brooklyn, NY," National Blue Ribbon Schools Program, available at https://nationalblueribbonschools.ed.gov/awardwinners/winning/17ny127pu_leadership_prep_ocean_hill_charter_school.html.

2. Patrick Lencioni, *The Five Dysfunctions of a Team* (San Francisco: Jossey-Bass, 2002).

Index

Page references followed by *fig* indicate an illustrated figure.

curriculum development, 81; practicing the seven levers of, 166; as primer on seven levers of leadership of, 6, 17–26; on principals impacted by Teresa Khirallah, 158; See It. Name It. Do It. unifying framework of the, 22–23; showing that bite-sized action step produces the quicker growth, 31; similarity of *PM's Guide to Leverage Leadership 2.0* action steps to those in, 31; Student Culture workshop from, 38; Weekly Data Meeting one-pager from, 40; on what an effective rollout should look like, 130–131

Leverage leadership model: introducing the seven levers of leadership, 20–22; a primer on the, 6, 17–26; student culture rehearsal super-lever (August 2017) example of using the, 17–18; Weekly Data Meeting (October 2017) example of using the, 18. *See also* See It. Name It. Do It. framework

Leverage leadership primer: on building a monthly map, 25–26; on building a weekly schedule, 24–25; on learning the levers, 23; lifting the super-levers, 17–19; on receiving coaching throughout the year, 26; on the See It. Name It. Do It. framework, 22–23

Leverage Leadership Sequence of Action Steps for Principals: on data-driven instruction (DDI), 45–49, 120–124; how to coach for success using the, 45–66; how to use the, 37; on observation and feedback, 55–57; overview of the, 33–35; on planning,

58–60; on professional development (PD), 60–64; on staff culture, 64–66; on student culture, 49–55. *See also* Action steps; Coaching; Principals

Leverage Leadership Sequence of Action Steps for Principals steps: 1. start the year with culture, 37; 2. focus first on the super-levers, 37; 3. keep it narrow, 37; applying to the four case studies, 37

Levers: building a data dashboard that focuses on the, 100; introduction to cultural levers, 5, 21; introduction to instructional levers, 5, 21; introduction to the seven levers of leadership, 20–22; keep the focus on the super-levers, 200; leading professional development (PD) using the, 166. *See also* Cultural levers; Instructional levers

Lofthus, Hannah: coach by meeting approach used by, 138–141; coach by walking approach used by, 136–138; her understanding of student culture, 128–130; monitoring student culture using rubric built by, 133, 136; publicly supporting her school leaders, 199; significant success of, 2, 203; on training the student culture rollout, 130; video clip 9: Do It—Practice Clinic (not on DVD), 128–129; video clip 11: See It and Name It, 131–132; video clip 14: See It and Name It (Coach by Meeting), 139–140; video clip 15: Do It (Coach by Meeting), 140

Principals: coaching teams of, 157–171; great teaching is made possible by great, 2–3. *See also* Action steps; Leverage Leadership Sequence of Action Steps for Principals

Professional development (PM): build data-driven instruction systems with, 200; description of the lever, 5, 21; include DDI as part of the, 88–89; lead PD of your vision, 65; the *Leverage Leadership 2.0* framework for, 166–170; Leverage Leadership Sequence of Action Steps for Principals, 60–64; lock in team time and, 182–183; materials included in this book on, 11; practice *Leverage Leadership 2.0*, 166; rollout on data-driven instruction, 88; See It. Name It. Do It. framework used for, 166–170; the seven levers used for, 166

Professional development videos: clip 17: Corburn—Do It (Plan)—Leading PD, 168–169; clip 18: Dowling—Do It (Practice)—Leading PD, 170

Professional development workshops: Data-Driven Instruction for Principal Managers, 208–217; Leading Student Culture for Principal Managers, 218–224; overview of the, 207–208

Pulling the Lever—Action Planning Worksheets: Action Steps for Principals, 66–68; Coaching Principals as a Team, 170–171; Coaching Principals on Data-Driven Instruction, 9–10, 124–125; Coaching Principals on Student Culture, 155–156; Finding the Time, 192–193. *See also* Coaching

Work, 93–104; coach by doing by monitoring, 110–114; coaching student culture by getting close to, 127–130; monitoring the learning and not just the process of, 98; samples available on the DVD, 93, 94–95; Weekly Data Meeting Leading Teacher Teams to Analyze Student Daily Work, 84–87

Student work analysis: create a cheat sheet for, 103–104; issues to consider for, 102–103; start with student work and not pedagogy, 103

Student work samples: School D Sample Student Work, 94–95; School F Sample Student Work, 96; School H Sample Student Work, 96

Students: Laura Garza's goals for her, 19; monitoring student culture by monitoring, 136

Success conditions: building data-driven instruction systems, 196, 199–200; a guide for creating, 77, 195–202; maximizing time in schools, 196–199; provide flexible support for turnarounds, 196, 200–201

Superintendents: Action Planning Worksheet for A Superintendent's Guide, 201–202; a guide for creating the conditions for success, 77, 195–202; how they should read this book, 12–13; publicly supporting school leaders, 199

Systems: big project time management, 184–185; building data-driven instruction, 196, 199–200; building

your weekly schedule, 24–25, 177–186; learning to build a schedule and district-wide, 6; principal managers cannot afford to do without, 191; task management, 187–191. *See also* Scheduling

T

The Talent Code (Coyle), 31

Task management: issues to consider for, 187–188; Serena's Weekly Task List, 189–191; set the focus for each quarter for, 188–189; Stop and Jot on, 191; for weekly tasks, 189–191

Teachers: coach by doing by using Name It, 112; make room for flexible hiring of, 200; monitoring student culture by monitoring, 136; Stop and Jot on Jesse's action to improve, 169; Weekly Data Meeting—Leading Teacher Teams to Analyze Student Daily Work, 86–87

Teaching: core idea on perfecting the plan to perfect the, 42; great principals make possible great, 2–3. *See also* Reteach lessons

Teaching Trust, 158

Testing: alignment of assessments to state, 78–79; DC PARCC Assessment: Percentage at or Above Proficiency in Math, 73*fig*; Missouri State Assessment: St. Louis Network 3 Schools, 29*fig*; Missouri State Assessment: Kaufman School Class of 2023, 129*fig*; New Jersey PARCC Assessment: Alexander Street School, 74*fig*; New Jersey PARCC

Worrell, Juliana: (*Continued*)
helping principals build weekly schedules for data meetings, 82; how she prepares her principal to lead a data meeting, 108–113; making sure schools have access to quality assessments, 77; making sure that staff knows the DDI basics, 88; refusing to define any school as failing, 73–74; significant success of, 2, 74–75, 203; student work analysis approach by, 102; video clip 3: See It (Gap)—Weekly Data Meeting, 108; video clip 4: See It and Name It—Weekly Data Meetings, 108; video clip 5: Do It (Plan)—Weekly Data Meetings, 108; video clip 6: See It and Do It—Coach by Doing, 110; video clip 7: Name It—Coach by Doing, 112

Z

Zitta, Jeanine: her example of coaching, 27–28; significant success of, 2, 203; video clip 1: See It and Name It—Manager Feedback Meeting, 28